"This book is free of both handwringing gloom and fist-pumping boosterism. Some of the most respected leaders in Christian higher education see with clarity the obstacles facing Christian colleges and universities, but see just as clearly the path forward. If we pay attention to the vision behind this book, the future of Christian higher education will be better than we've ever dared to hope."

—**Russell Moore**, *Editor-in-Chief*, Christianity Today

"Todd Ream and Jerry Pattengale articulate a foundational truth of Scripture, which they deftly place in dialogue with the teachings of Dietrich Bonhoeffer. They argue insightfully that current challenges to Christian institutions of higher education actually deepen and enliven the discipleship mandate that powers us. Ultimately, they remind leaders of Christian colleges and universities that we are faithfully Christian when and insofar as we come alongside the Church to fulfill our Lord's great disciple-making commission. Faithfulness to Jesus fulfills our mission, not programs or enrollment quotas. This book re-grounds us in our existential purpose. I will strongly recommend it to our board of trustees and to others."

—**Merle Stoltzfus**, *Chair of the Board of Trustees, LeTourneau University*

"In more recent decades, Christian colleges and universities have distinguished themselves by maintaining a strong sense of telos, an intellectual muscle and way of life that trickles down to all aspects of the college experience—including the graduates that are its most lasting fruit. But as survival mindsets have taken over in the last decade, even this most needed contribution to American civic life has been displaced. *The Anxious Middle* shakes off the dust, grounding the survival of these precious institutions not in the chess pieces of pragmatism, but in the discipleship that is their beginning, middle, and end."

—**Anne Snyder**, *Editor-in-Chief*, Comment

"Our time demands that Christian scholarship inform discipleship and, in turn, is informed by it. To bring the combined insight of St. Benedict, Dietrich Bonhoeffer, and the heirs of the Brethren of the Common Life into the conversation, is both appropriate and inspired. Christian scholarship contributes to public discourse only when Christ is its cantus firmus, for then it becomes profoundly humanist and culturally transformative."

—**John W. de Gruchy**, *Emeritus Professor of Christian Studies, University of Cape Town and Extraordinary Professor of Theology, Stellenbosch University*

"*The Anxious Middle* reminds Christian college leaders that we are ultimately preparing graduates for society and for heaven so we should be clear about our institutions' aspirations, expand our problem-solving imaginations, include God and diverse partners in our collaborations, and be thoughtful about how we can bring Christ-centered illumination to the broader culture."

—**Kimberly Battle-Walters Denu**, *Provost, Westmont College*

"Ream and Pattengale offer an invaluable map of the contemporary landscape of Christian higher education and, most importantly, a theological grounding for strategic and tactical decisions to move educational institutions forward with meaning and purpose. This work is especially recommended for administrators in Christian higher education who are looking to go beyond mere procedural adjustments to think carefully about the central purposes of their institutions as they consider the challenges and opportunities they face."

—**Joseph Creech**, *Director, Lilly Fellows Program*

"Christ-centered colleges and universities are in for a long, hard struggle. The social, financial, political, and reputational challenges we now face will be with us for the foreseeable future. The responses in *The Anxious Middle* are not merely tactical—adjustments to operating budgets, enrollment strategies, and the like—but strategically rooted in the broader narrative of redemption, from creation to consummation. Drawing on our best thinkers from Benedict to Bonhoeffer, they seek to nourish our collective mission by advocating for the spiritual, intellectual, and moral discipleship that is only possible at deeply Christian institutions of higher learning."

—**Philip Graham Ryken**, *President, Wheaton College*

"*The Anxious Middle* is the one new book you must read if you are connected to Christian higher education in any way. Ream and Pattengale make a bold and correct claim that the future of Christian higher education lies in understanding the 'why' it should exist. And that 'why' is the discipleship of the student into a firm belief that God is the creator of all things and therefore God is at the center of all things. Once you know the 'why,' presidents, university leaders, faculty, and board members will be able to shape and give oversight to all the other important and necessary functions of the university. *The Anxious Middle* supports its thesis with an engrossing discussion of Bonhoffer's life and writings. Throughout the book the practical functions of a university are woven into historical context and vice versa. If you are a newcomer or a seasoned professional to Christian higher education, this book will equip to imagine a future by knowing the past."

—**Shirley Hoogstra**, *President, Council for Christian Colleges and Universities*

"*The Anxious Middle* lays out a compelling vision for how Christian colleges and universities can embrace the opportunities this historical moment provides, and effectively cultivate discipleship, collaboration, and generosity in the Christian leaders of tomorrow. Research increasingly shows that religion is important to human flourishing, and so we need to attend to the health of our religious institutions. Ream and Pattengale point the way toward a future of vibrant Christian higher education, encouraging us to draw on religion's powerful ability to harness meaning and purpose in pursuit of flourishing."

—**Heather Templeton Dill**, *President, John Templeton Foundation*

"In the present torrent of threatening opposition to Christian traditions, Christian values, and Christian colleges, this book charges into the fray and reaches down into the murky mission drift of compromise with the strong arm of historical insight to pull Christian colleges up into the warm light of renewal. Its profound yet simple and supernatural remedy to the ails of Christian higher education is the courageous return to our founding principles, indeed, our singular, radical, founding Principle—the person, Jesus Christ. Herein it is proposed that becoming again pure disciples of Jesus and committed ambassadors of his gospel can establish our Christian colleges as outposts of the kingdom where our students can experience the life-giving power of God on earth as it is in heaven. May we have the courage to engage in this invitation."

—**Jim Gash**, *President, Pepperdine University*

"For anyone interested in the state of and possibilities for Christian higher education, Todd Ream and Jerry Pattengale offer an invaluable guide in their new work *The Anxious Middle*. Both aspirational and deeply practical, *The Anxious Middle* explores the theological vision and guiding principles of a faith-grounded education, as well as innovative approaches and strategies for pursuing it."

—**Cherie Harder**, *President, The Trinity Forum*

"Ream and Pattengale have raised expectations with such an ambitious title. And they do not disappoint. This book is not simply about education, it is an education. It is a catechesis to answer the question, 'What is the chief end of education?' While they explore higher education, they have given us a key to unlock a treasure for churches and institutions called to disciple people and communities in Christlikeness. Get this book and let its wisdom reanimate your vision for how people can be formed anew in our day."

—**Walter Kim**, *President, National Association of Evangelicals*

"Ream and Pattengale have rightly identified that in order for our institutions of higher education to be forces of change for the common good, they need to have a 'why' big enough to support the 'how.' In this book, the authors help leaders ask the critical 'why' and 'how' questions. By focusing on the core principles that organizations on all sides of these issues need to consider, the book creates space for those of varying perspectives to engage these ideas without sacrificing their own beliefs or priorities. If taken seriously and acted upon, these questions will drive the type of thoughtful, diverse innovation that is needed to propel Christian higher education into the future—even into, if we are bold enough to hope for it, a new season of flourishing."

—**Romanita Hairston**, *Chief Executive Officer, M.J. Murdock Charitable Trust*

The Anxious Middle

Planning for the Future of the Christian College

Todd C. Ream and Jerry Pattengale

Foreword by Mark A. Noll

Postscripts by Jon S. Kulaga, Linda A. Livingstone, and Beck A. Taylor

BAYLOR UNIVERSITY PRESS

Cover design by theBookDesigners
Cover art: Flandrin, Hippolyte (1809–1864) / French, Christ's entrance to Jerusalem on Palm Sunday: the inhabitants greet him with joy by spreading their clothes on the floor, wielding olive branches. Detail of a fresco by Hypolithe [Hippolyte] Flandrin (1809–1864), 19th century, Church of Saint Germain des Pres, Paris. Photo © Photo Josse / Bridgeman Images
Book design by Elyxandra Encarnación for Baylor University Press

Library of Congress Cataloging-in-Publication Data

Names: Ream, Todd C., author. | Pattengale, Jerry A. author. | Noll, Mark A., 1946- author of foreword.
Title: The anxious middle : planning for the future of the Christian college / Todd C. Ream, Jerry Pattengale ; foreword Mark A. Noll ; postscripts by Jon S. Kulaga, Linda A. Livingstone, and Beck A. Taylor.
Description: Waco : Baylor University Press, 2023. | Includes index. | Summary: "Engages Dietrich Bonhoeffer's writings and Western Christian history to offer resources and strategies for Christian colleges and universities to address the current crisis of Christian higher education"-- Provided by publisher.
Identifiers: LCCN 2023025239 (print) | LCCN 2023025240 (ebook) | ISBN 9781481318501 (hardback) | ISBN 9781481318532 (adobe pdf) | ISBN 9781481318525 (epub)
Subjects: LCSH: Bonhoeffer, Dietrich, 1906-1945. | Christian universities and colleges.
Classification: LCC LC538 .R43 2023 (print) | LCC LC538 (ebook) | DDC 378/.071--dc23/eng/20230804
LC record available at https://lccn.loc.gov/2023025239
LC ebook record available at https://lccn.loc.gov/2023025240

Dedicated to the Memory of

David L. Riggs

Scholar, Teacher, Father, Husband,
& Servant of Jesus Christ

*For now we see in a mirror dimly, but then face to face.
Now I know in part; then I shall understand fully, even as I
have been fully understood.*
                                        —1 Corinthians 13:12 (RSV)

Contents

Foreword

Mark A. Noll
Professor of History Emeritus, University of Notre Dame

W ith particularly apt phrasing, Todd Ream and Jerry Pattengale address the challenges of contemporary Christian higher education by describing how the "tailwinds" that propelled multidimensional growth since the 1970s have in the recent past become "headwinds." Although they do not obsess in describing those headwinds, even their brief sketch is sobering: economic uncertainties, political polarization, the fallout from COVID-19, a shrinking pool of potential applicants, the general secularization of society, and looming governmental insistence on accommodating alternative lifestyles. After viewing such a list, readers might expect a book titled *The Anxious Middle* to respond as Vladimir Lenin responded early in the twentieth century when his fragile band of Marxists faced, as he put it, "burning questions for our movement." Immediately, Lenin focused on prescribing "what is to be done."

Instead, however, Ream and Pattengale begin with what looks like a meandering detour. They want readers to go back in time to the winter of 1932–1933 when Dietrich Bonhoeffer was offering lectures on the early chapters of Genesis that would later be published under the title *Creation and Fall.* (Not incidentally, Bonhoeffer delivered these lectures in Germany at a time of crisis far more fateful for his nation and its churches than anything facing Christian educators today. Even as he lectured, Adolf Hitler was securing his hold on the reins of Germany's government, a tipping point that would lead eventually to the all-out devastation of world war.)

Moreover, as this book addresses the constituencies with a stake in Christian higher education, it reaches even further back into the past. Implausible as it may seem, the authors want readers to understand how light from the ancient *Rule of St. Benedict* (fifth century) and the reforming Brethren of the Common Life (fifteenth century) might illuminate the path for Christian college administrators, as well as for students at their institutions, their parents, alumni, and interested third parties.

To be sure, there is also a great deal of sage practical advice in the pages that follow. Under the heading "Imagination," the authors urge creative thinking to realize a full range of possibilities for making higher education both intellectually stimulating and practically relevant. They hold up "Collaboration" as an ideal for faculty to set aside nervous turf protection of their own disciplines for dedicated exploration of ways showing how the humanities, the sciences, the social sciences, the arts, business, and professional training actually depend on each other. Under the heading "Illumination," they underscore how imperative it has become for educators to work intentionally at communicating the fruits of academic labor beyond the campus.

But before it considers "Imagination," "Collaboration," and "Illumination," the book begins by considering "Aspiration," or founding principles for the entire project of Christian higher education. For that purpose, Ream and Pattengale find what

Bonhoeffer wrote in *Creation and Fall* uniquely applicable as an ideal place to begin. As he expounded Genesis 1–4:1, Bonhoeffer stressed that all things have been created by God, that God sustains the creation at every moment and in every place, and that the fullest manifestation of God's purpose for humanity is found in the person and work of Jesus Christ. Inspired by Bonhoeffer's vision, Ream and Pattengale insist that in order to accomplish the purposes for which it aspires, properly Christian higher education must begin with a similar theological vision. More than the practical suggestions that the book eventually delivers, they want readers to grasp that, if Christian colleges and universities are to be saved, they will be saved through the outworking of Christian discipleship. Their exploration of the many facets of such discipleship drives the entire book.

As it happens, another part of Dietrich Bonhoeffer's life story reinforces this message. It concerns what he wrote after making two extended visits to the United States in the 1930s. Shortly after the second visit in 1939, a decision to leave the refuge he was offered, and his return to the German-church struggle against Hitler, Bonhoeffer wrote a particularly perceptive essay about what he had seen of American Christian life. In the essay, he expressed wonder at the dynamic impact of the American churches on so many aspects of the nation's social life. For someone raised in a Europe that clung to the institutions of formal church establishment, he admired what commitment to religious freedom had made possible in the United States. While that admiration extended to all American churches, he was most impressed with the African American churches he had witnessed in New York City and the American South; even where America's vaunted "freedom" was more hypocritical than actual, the black churches provided entire communities with self-confidence, stability, and hope.

Yet along with positive recognition of what American churches *did*, Bonhoeffer also registered serious criticism. Is it possible, he wondered, that in the profusion of activity that

**characterized American church life, Americans had lost sight
of the Christian gospel itself? He put it like this:**

> American theology and the American church as a whole
> have never been able to understand the meaning of "crit-
> icism" by the Word of God and all that signifies. . . . In
> American theology, Christianity is still essentially religion
> and ethics. But because of this, the person and work of
> Jesus Christ must, for theology, sink into the background
> and in the long run remain misunderstood, because it is
> not recognized as the sole ground of radical judgment and
> radical forgiveness.[1]

Bonhoeffer never had the opportunity to expand on these observations. Yet as Ream and Pattengale unfold the insights of Bonhoeffer's earlier book, they in effect particularize the message of his
1939 essay. Instead of "radical judgment and radical forgiveness,"
they want readers to view "radical discipleship" as the orienting
value—the only essential orientation—for Christian higher education. And so *The Anxious Middle*, brimful as it is with practical
advice for meeting contemporary challenges, is first a call resem-
bling what St. Augustine famously heard at a crisis point in his own
life. When the voice of a child rang out, "tolle, lege" (pick it up and
read it), Augustine opened the Scriptures to read from the thir-
teenth chapter of the Epistle to the Romans. As he saw there the
Pauline admonition to "put on the Lord Jesus Christ," so too this
book urges all who pick it up to realize the potential of Christian
higher education by first "putting on the Lord Jesus Christ."

Acknowledgments

The genesis of the ideas in this book stem back to the earliest days of our respective callings to the Christian academic vocation. As the place the Church does its thinking, the Christian college plays a critical role in preparing the next generation of leaders while modeling the intellectual as well as the moral and theological virtues that the pursuit of truth demands.

Both of us were fortunate to attend Christian colleges. We wrote this book in the hope of securing a future for the Christian college that not only matches the depth of disciple-making experiences we encountered but ideally exceeds them. With that end in mind, we pray the theological imaginations exercised by the individuals who follow us in relation to this topic are greater than the imaginations we exercised here.

The present season, however, leaves us more aware of the challenges that come when living in the anxious middle than any other season we experienced since embracing those callings. In fall 2021, *Christianity Today*'s Andy Olsen asked one of us to consider revisiting the magazine's March 2012 cover story, "How to Save the Christian College." Despite the insights our friend Perry

Glanzer offered in that issue, "the times they are [still] a-changin.'" Shameful election cycles, social unrest, a pandemic, and financial uncertainty, to name only four, prompted Andy's query. While we were initially incapable of offering a remotely suitable response, you now see our "article" exceeds in word count anything a reasonable magazine editor would consider.

While on that journey toward offering this response, we were fortunate that friends and colleagues with the kinds of theological imaginations we previously noted were willing to join us. As evidence of the power of ecumenical relations and the unity that Christ's body is called to reflect, the first two people who wrestled with an outline of the ideas that worked their way into this book were Notre Dame's John C. Cavadini and Boston College's Michael J. James. The two of them think more deeply about Catholic higher education than anyone else we are privileged to call friends. Their responses to Bonhoeffer's work gave proof to the possibility that one of Protestantism's saints may have something to offer—especially during this season.

As the manuscript developed, Notre Dame's George Marsden, Samford's Paul House, the Episcopal School of Jacksonville's Andrew Deskins, and Notre Dame's Tony Oleck challenged us to think in ways that defied the distinction all too often plaguing academic work—theory and practice. Their insights thus helped us strive toward what theology is intended to offer—the language of lived Christianity.

To their credit, three Christian college presidents were willing to share this manuscript with members of their respective boards to help us consider whether what we offered was an aid toward lived Christianity. We are thus honored to list Houghton's Wayne Lewis, Covenant's Derek Halvorson, and LeTourneau's Steve Mason as individuals to whom we owe a great debt of gratitude. We hope the time they spent reading the manuscript was also of service to the leadership they offer their institutions.

A group of graduate students graciously allowed a portion of their higher education leadership course to be focused on a penultimate draft of this book. Jireh Bagyendera, Alyssa Bates, Sarah Chipka, Sarah Hagelberger, Kizito Kakule Mayao, Aidan Reichard, and Emma Sachsenmaier offered insights only individuals preparing to invest in these questions on a daily basis could offer. To her credit, Emma Sachsenmaier then made another read of the manuscript and offered feedback that greatly improved the quality of what it strived to offer. By the time this book is in print, all of them will be living with these questions in their own ways. We hope we served them as well as they served us.

Two editors, one a long-standing friend and one a new friend, invested heavily in this project and helped it become more than we envisioned. In terms of a long-standing friend, Evelyn Bence has edited our work for the better part of a decade. As with other projects, she kept us not only out of the grammatical weeds but also out of the theological ones. For these reasons, we offered her the title of *Editor Extraordinaire*.

In terms of a new friend, Baylor University Press' Cade Jarrell believed in this manuscript from the very beginning. He helped us refine our idea, be patient, and stay on task. With his guidance, we grew in confidence we could offer something worthy of a reader's time and energy as well as the planning processes designed to chart a future for the Christian college.

Two professional communities continue to enrich our lives and our ability to grapple with the breadth and depth of the high calling that is the Christian academic vocation. For over fifty years, *Christian Scholar's Review* has served as one of the leading journals focused on ways the Christian faith informs learning across the disciplines. We count it a privilege to play roles leading that journal during this season and hope what we pass on to our successors is a faithful reflection of the fiduciary responsibility we inherited from our predecessors. To that end, we are fortunate to call Margaret Diddams, Perry Glanzer, John Hwang, Steve

Oldham, and Todd Steen friends and colleagues. In their own ways, they greatly contributed to what is offered in these pages.

For over one hundred years, Indiana Wesleyan University has sought to be "a Christ-centered academic community committed to changing the world by developing students in character, scholarship, and leadership." Such a community added greatly to our sense of the importance of the calling we accepted and, when practiced well in the light of God's grace, the impact that calling can have on the next generation. Hundreds of colleagues and students implicitly contributed to the impressions we offer in these pages. Explicitly, Chris Devers, Jim Vermilya, Jeff Tabone, and David Wright shared insights we otherwise would have missed when seeking to communicate those impressions. We are thus grateful for their time, those insights, and their support as they walked alongside us through the completion of this project.

Any opportunity to work with Notre Dame's Mark Noll is a blessing. Few people exerted greater influence on perceptions of the Christian life of the mind than Mark over the course of his distinguished career. Such an impact obviously comes through his written works, including, most recently, his two-volume history of the Bible in American culture. If you were to ask Mark where he placed his greatest emphasis when exerting that influence, however, we would estimate he would say he placed it on shaping his students as scholars, teachers, and servants of Jesus Christ. We are thus grateful he was willing to open this book by contributing the foreword.

When striving to make sure this book proved not only theologically insightful but useful to people who live with the pressures of planning for the future of the Christian college daily, we thought inviting three university presidents to add their insights would serve readers well. Despite the incredible demands on their time, Indiana Wesleyan's Jon Kulaga, Baylor's Linda Livingstone, and Samford's Beck Taylor graciously accepted our invitations. As a result, their words add a level of depth to what we proposed in these pages that only the experiences and wisdom represented by the four of them could offer.

As we have been blessed to note over the course of our careers, our greatest debt of gratitude is owed to our wives and children. With Sara, Todd raised two daughters—Addison and Ashley—who are benefiting from their time at Wheaton College and Westmont College, respectively. With Cindy, Jerry raised four sons—Jason, Josh, Nick, and Mike—who benefited from the years they spent as students at Indiana Wesleyan University. In their own ways, all of them provided us with support and encouragement for which we will always be grateful. We hope the words we offer in this book are worthy not only of their educations but of the educations of all children who chose a Christian college and the love of the families who support them.

While we were completing this book, on August 9, 2022, David L. Riggs went to stand beside his Lord and Savior. He was fifty-six and still looked like the all-star tight end from his playing days at Azusa Pacific University. His greatest joy in life emanated from the love he shared with his wife, Laura, and the love they shared with their four children—Patrick, Christian, Alexandra, and Faith. A bout with COVID-19 six weeks earlier left him with a blood clot and an unexpected and sudden death that stunned his family, the College Wesleyan Church community, and the Indiana Wesleyan University community.

"Riggs," as his friends and colleagues often called him, earned graduate degrees from Princeton Theological Seminary and the University of Oxford's Christ Church. He was then appointed dean of Indiana Wesleyan University's John Wesley Honors College, the only position he held over the course of his career. He loved Augustine and the church fathers and was a brilliant student of Latin, a deep yet agile thinker, and a committed mentor. As a result, David was a pillar of the National Collegiate Honors Council and Society for Classical Studies but, like the Benedictines, was resolved to give his life to one community.

As Bonhoeffer challenges us, Christian higher education is first about discipleship. While leading the John Wesley Honors College, David discipled hundreds of men and women into meaningful lives of service to Christ. Such experiences compel us to champion Christian higher education, to spend time reflecting on what Bonhoeffer has to say to us as we live in the anxious middle, and to plan for the future all the while awaiting Christ's return. In that spirit, we dedicate this volume to David.

Todd C. Ream, Greentown, Indiana
Jerry Pattengale, Marion, Indiana

Introduction

Life in the Anxious Middle (*Again*)

> *Until I die, I'll sing these songs*
> *On the shores of Babylon*
> *Still looking for a home*
> *In a world where I belong*
>
> From Switchfoot's "Where I Belong"
> Vice Verses, *Atlantic Records, 2011*

Spring 1970 was arguably the most tumultuous season in the history of American higher education. On April 30, the Nixon administration announced the expansion of the military campaign in Vietnam into Cambodia, prompting even larger numbers of students to raise their voices in opposition. On May 4, Ohio National Guard troops opened fire on protesters gathered at Kent State University, killing four and wounding nine. Afraid they could not keep their respective students safe, administrators serving more than three hundred campuses across the country canceled the remaining weeks in the spring semester and sent students home.

Amid that anxious season, fourteen professors from different Christian colleges gathered that May at Wheaton College to discuss the transition of an intra-institutional publication known as *The Gordon Review* to the interinstitutional publication now known as *Christian Scholar's Review* (*CSR*). According to George M. Marsden, an attendee at that meeting, "[We] saw a need for exchange

1

of views among Christian scholars, especially at their institutions. [We] gained just enough funding from a number of interested Christian colleges to keep the enterprise afloat in its early years."[1] In fall 2021, during another tumultuous season in American higher education, *CSR* celebrated its fiftieth anniversary, now firmly established as a leading journal of Christian scholarship.[2]

If one way to mark the formal emergence of what is known today as Christian scholarship is by tracing it to the establishment of *CSR* in 1970, one way to mark the formal emergence of the Christian college movement is to trace it to the formation of the Christian College Consortium in 1971.[3] As the rate of secularization accelerated on mainline Protestant college and university campuses, thirteen evangelical schools came together to support one another in their commitment "to the centrality of Christ and the full exploration of the meaning and implications of faithful scholarship."[4] In 1975, Wheaton's Arthur F. Holmes published what arguably became the most definitive description of those institutions in *The Idea of a Christian College*.

In 1976, an additional network of Christian colleges and universities was established and is known today as the Council for Christian Colleges and Universities (CCCU).[5] Now with approximately 180 member institutions in some twenty countries, "the CCCU's mission is to advance the cause of Christ-centered higher education and to help our institutions transform lives by faithfully relating scholarship and service to biblical truth."[6]

Although individual Christian colleges and universities would face a wide array of challenges over the next forty-five years, that period of time was one of enormous growth by almost any qualitative and quantitative indicators. For example, not only would the quality and quantity of articles submitted to *CSR* increase, but discipline-based associations—such as the Conference on Christianity and Literature, the Conference on Faith and History, and the Society of Christian Philosophers—flourished. Today some forty Christian professional societies sponsor approximately twenty discipline-specific journals.

Over the course of the same period, many Christian colleges and universities would witness record growth in students and employees. For example, an editorial in the April 1999 issue of *Christianity Today* titled "Why Christian Colleges Are Booming" noted "undergraduate enrollments and the 94 CCCU schools have grown 24 percent from 1990–1996, more than four times than enrollment growth at private institutions."[7] That editorial then went on to note that "What is most important to most students attending Christian colleges are valuable course content and excellent instruction in their majors and knowledgeable faculty."[8]

Toward the latter half of the 2000s, the tailwinds to which Christian colleges and universities became accustomed switched to headwinds of which at least four prove noteworthy. First, the "Great Recession" (2008) caused families to be much more cautious in terms of debt, including educational debt. Children who watched so many of their parents lose positions opted in larger numbers for majors, such as business and engineering, perceived as being more immediately translatable to employment opportunities than majors in the arts and humanities.

In previous decades, tuition at both public and private universities had also grown at record rates. The combination of the perceived value of a college education and an age of relative financial prosperity led many students and their families to take out loans and do so with some confidence. The recession understandably led students and families to think of higher education as job training and of cost as a leading variable in their decision making.[9] As a result, admissions officers grew accustomed to financial aid packages rather than awards being the starting point for negotiations. Academic administrators grew receptive to offering majors and minors responsive to market pressures rather than relying on a historically determined canon of learning defined by its formative value.

Second, declines in populations in certain regions of the United States as well as a decline in the birthrate stemming back to the 2008 recession meant a reduction in the college-bound pool of students. Such declines are predicted to be greatest in the

Northeast and the Midwest, regions with an abundance of colleges and universities—particularly liberal arts colleges and universities founded in response to movements such as the Second Great Awakening. Nationwide, demographers predict that, by 2025, colleges and universities will see as much as a 15 percent decrease in students.[10]

In advance of such a drop in student enrollment, colleges and universities that believe they are more susceptible are investing in at least two strategies. To begin, in an effort to increase the financial solvency of their respective institutions, administrators are eliminating unnecessary costs, maximizing existing revenue streams, and, where possible, identifying new revenue streams. Depending on the in-kind resources an institution may already possess, covering the start-up costs for new revenue streams often puts greater pressure on institutions to maximize existing revenue streams and eliminate unnecessary costs—precipitating a spiral yielding a host of predictable, yet unintended, consequences.

In addition, when combined with the mounting perception that financial aid packages are negotiable, administrators often find themselves increasing the discount rate to maintain perceptions of financial solvency. For example, the National Association of College and University Business Officers' "2021 Tuition Discounting Study" noted a record high of a 54.5 percent tuition discount rate for first-year students attending private colleges and universities and a record high of 49 percent for all students attending private colleges and universities.[11] For institutions with resources such as large endowments, such efforts are sustainable. For others, perception and reality will eventually part ways.

Third, the passage of the Affordable Care Act in 2010 raised concerns about whether the federal government would compel Christian colleges and universities to cover contraception, abortifacients, and/or abortive practices deemed in opposition to their religious convictions. To be clear, very few Christian college and university leaders lobbied against the need for a reform of the health care system. Their concerns, in contrast, resided with the details of such legislation and, in particular, mandates the federal government might impose related to what practices and prescriptive services would be deemed required in terms of the provision of health care.[12]

In contrast to mainline Protestants, evangelicals retained an opposition to practices such as abortion. Such opposition then informed provisions offered to employees as well as students. Catholic colleges and universities were among the first to question what employers might be required to offer, with evangelical colleges and universities eventually following suit. In an expression of ecumenical solidarity, Catholic University of America and Wheaton College filed a joint lawsuit in 2012 against the U.S. Department of Health and Human Services (HHS) "because the HHS mandate requiring the college to provide and subsidize insurance coverage for abortion-inducing drugs violates the conscience of the school and its members, and denies their First Amendment freedom of religion."[13]

Fourth, the U.S. Supreme Court's 2015 decision in *Obergefell v. Hodges* raised concerns about whether the federal government would compel Christian colleges and universities to hire employees who disagree in principle and/or practice with an institution's views on sexuality and marriage. Such a decision also raised concerns about whether codes of conduct between students that affirmed sexuality as being a practice between one married man and one married woman would hold. Several mainline Protestant denominations approved same-sex unions before the *Obergefell* decision. The United Church of Christ (Congregationalists), for example, voted in favor of same-sex unions in 2005.[14] The Episcopal Church USA approved a liturgy for such unions in 2012.[15]

In contrast, most evangelicals retained a view of marriage as being between one man and one woman and that sexuality, when practiced, was within such a context. Although pressure against such a view was mounting prior to *Obergefell*, public debates became more frequent after that decision with pressure coming from both students and faculty. Students on a number of campuses raised their voices in person and in print opposing traditional views. Some faculty have also raised their voices; others have gone so far as to officiate same-sex unions. Despite these headwinds, Christian colleges and universities as a whole are still stronger by almost any measure than at almost any point in their respective histories. Over the course of the past forty-five years, many of their enrollments, operating budgets, and endowments grew to record levels. Facilities were added, and existing facilities were updated. Institutions rose in various rankings, and their faculty grew in pedagogical strength, scholarly acumen, and public platform. While positive, those advances created scenarios by which Christian colleges and universities proved more sensitive to various market pressures while also making them worthy of greater public interest and scrutiny. As our predecessors with *Christian Scholar's Review* did in the early 1970s, we seek to challenge Christian colleges and universities to think anew about what may grow out of this anxious season.

Considering the fact that we live in what Dietrich Bonhoeffer in *Creation and Fall* called the "anxious middle"—somewhere between Eden and the Apocalypse—the pressures facing Christian colleges and universities are both existential and practical. To confront those challenges but embrace opportunities that may also be present, Christian colleges and universities need to employ in their planning processes a fourfold approach, as evident in the titles of our four subsequent chapters. Such an approach will compel institutions to be articulate about their missions, imaginative in advancing them, collaborative in deploying them, and strategic in sharing them.

Defining these efforts clearly and with a resulting confidence should reach back into each institution's heritage. Definitions need clear plans for discipleship that reflect the school's unique history and the spirit of the age in which it finds itself serving Christ and his kingdom. At this point, Bonhoeffer's *Creation and Fall* serves as a useful guide for at least three reasons.

First, the value in turning to Bonhoeffer is born out of the authority evangelicals grant him as a theologian. In his essay in *Bonhoeffer, Christ, and Culture*, Timothy Larsen argued "that for evangelicals today Dietrich Bonhoeffer is the most widely cited and respected theologian of the last four hundred years or more since the era of the Protestant Reformers."[16] Regardless of how evangelicals identify themselves in this polarized age, that appeal for Bonhoeffer holds—an appeal that seemingly knows no theological, sociological, or political boundaries.

Second, *Creation and Fall*, one of Bonhoeffer's comparatively undercited works, is of great relevance to the focus of this project. Inspired by Karl Barth's groundbreaking theological exegesis of Romans, Bonhoeffer offers in *Creation and Fall* a theological appraisal of the significance of the first three chapters of Genesis.[17] Bonhoeffer joined Karl Barth in breaking ranks from scholars focused on historical and literary explorations of the Bible when offering lectures at the University of Berlin in the winter term of 1932–1933. In contrast, Bonhoeffer "was above all intensely concerned with the question: How can these words live?"[18] As a result, Bonhoeffer believed Genesis 1–4:1, as with all Scripture, "had to be read in the light of God's self-disclosure in Jesus Christ."[19]

Finally, Bonhoeffer's desire to explore the theological significance of Genesis 1–4:1 occurred during an era when life in the anxious middle was not only palpable but perhaps more pressing than in almost any other season in history. For much of Bonhoeffer's life, the German Republic wrestled with the physical and existential realities brought on by the defeat it had experienced during World War I. Every quality of the once-proud nation, arguably the apex of Western culture in the 1800s and early 1900s, was called into question. That abrupt unmooring of identity created the conditions in the winter of 1932 and 1933 during which the National Socialist Party came to power.

In *The Rise and Fall of the Third Reich*, William L. Shirer noted that "the Third Reich owed nothing to the fortunes of war, or to foreign influence. It was inaugurated in peacetime, and peacefully, by the Germans themselves, out of both their weaknesses and their strengths. The Germans imposed the Nazi tyranny on themselves."[20] That pending imposition lived with Bonhoeffer while he was delivering the lectures that comprise *Creation and Fall* and eventually cost Bonhoeffer his life. By turning to Genesis 1–4:1, Bonhoeffer believed Scripture offered an understanding of how Christians were to live—to live in the anxious middle and do so, as many other members of Christ's body did before them, even unto death.

* * *

The primary audience for this volume includes leaders—trustees, administrators, and faculty members—serving Christian colleges and universities in the anxious middle. Each of the four chapters defining this book concludes with a variety of questions. These audience members can use those questions in various ways in theologically informed planning processes ranging from the university-wide to the department or program level.[21]

An additional audience for this volume includes students of higher education preparing to serve as administrators and/or faculty members along with the faculty members leading their classes and coordinating their research projects. This book is designed to be helpful as a textbook in courses such as leadership, organizational change, and strategic planning. While the guide to strategic planning may prove helpful to them over the course of their careers, we also hope the theologically informed way of thinking about higher education is a habit of mind that will endure.

A final audience for this volume includes officials representing a wide variety of denominations and nondenominational churches with interests in how Christian colleges and universities contribute to the health of the body of Christ. As denominational loyalties decline within evangelicalism, church leaders are grappling with the nature of the relationship they share with the colleges and universities they sponsor. This book is designed to be a resource to them as they consider that relationship, the trustees they appoint, and the expectations they communicate. An additional hope is that leaders of megachurches, churches that now often include large conglomerates of satellite churches, become more active in partnerships with Christian higher education and vice versa.

* * *

Reaching back to John Henry Newman's *The Idea of a University*, Christian colleges and universities have proven to be the focus of numerous titles. Inspired by Newman, perhaps no book proved more influential on Christian college and university campuses than Arthur F. Holmes' previously mentioned *The Idea of a Christian College* (1975; revised in 1987). An effort such as *The Idea of a Christian College: A Reexamination for Today's University* (2013) was inspired by Holmes' work. Those normative efforts, however valuable, do not directly engage with the present array of challenges and have slipped considerably in book sales in recent years.

Any overview of the related literature, however brief, would prove incomplete without mention of titles such as George M. Marsden's *The Soul of the American University: From Protestant Establishment to Established Nonbelief* (1994; revised in 2021) and Mark A. Noll's *The Scandal of the Evangelical Mind* (1995; revised in 2022). Although these works assess the threat posed by secularization and a historical account of the challenges and opportunities of intellectual life within evangelicalism, Marsden's revised edition points to how the challenges facing Christian colleges and universities changed since he wrote the original book.

The literature concerning higher education as a whole is replete with titles documenting challenges facing colleges and universities. Since the publication of Allan Bloom's *The Closing of the American Mind* (1987) and Bruce Wilshire's *The Moral Collapse of the University: Professionalism, Purity, and Alienation* (1989), critiques of higher education have become almost as fashionable as apocalyptic. A brief sample of titles published over the course of the past thirty years includes Bill Readings' *The University in Ruins* (1997), Harry R. Lewis' *Excellence without a Soul: How a Great University Forgot Education* (2006), and Anthony T. Kronman's *Education's*

End: Why Our Colleges and Universities Have Given Up on the Meaning of Life (2007). The most recent titles in this genre are represented by Jason Brennan and Philip Magness' *Cracks in the Ivory Tower: The Moral Mess of Higher Education* (2019), Ronald G. Musto's *The Attack on Higher Education: The Dissolution of the American University* (2021), and Will Bunch's *After the Ivory Tower Falls: How College Broke Up the American Dream and Blew Up Our Politics—and How to Fix It* (2022).

Embodying a more hopeful approach, a handful of noted scholars focused their energies on this topic in what may be the final books of their careers. For example, in 2022, Wendy Fischman (a project director for Harvard University's Graduate School of Education) and Howard Gardner (the Hobbs Research Professor at Harvard University) published *The Real World of College: What Higher Education Is and What It Can Be*. While optimistic about its future, Fischman and Gardner are clear-eyed about the challenges facing higher education. In particular, they note, "The sector [higher education] has lost its way and stands in considerable peril."[22] In order to find their way, Fischman and Howard argue that "campuses need a laser-like focus on the academic mission of higher education."[23] Far from being monolithic, that mission should serve the institution's "civic, ethical, religious, or vocational orientation."[24]

Later in 2022, Richard J. Light (the Carl H. Pforzheimer Professor at Harvard University) and Allison Jegla (a higher-education strategist) published *Becoming Great Universities: Small Steps for Sustained Excellence*. Amid the challenges facing higher education, Light and Jegla contend "that when campus culture signals to each person at a university that they have a special opportunity to make a positive difference and to enhance the 'common good' at their campus, such a culture is especially productive."[25]

Although critique far outweighs the proposed solutions found in these titles, a growing number of titles focus on the opportunities beginning to appear. Perhaps the most prominent representatives of the authors of these titles are Michael M. Crow and William B. Dabars with *Designing the New American University* (2015) and *The Fifth Wave: The Evolution of American Higher Education* (2020). Other recent titles include John Schmalzbauer and Kathleen L. Mahoney's *The Resilience of Religion in American Higher Education* (2018), Joshua Kim and Edward J. Maloney's *Learning Innovation and the Future of Higher Education* (2020), and Bryan Alexander's *Academia Next: The Futures of Higher Education* (2020).

No book currently addresses the growing number of challenges and opportunities facing Christian colleges and universities. As a result, what follows builds upon the literature concerning those institutions, acknowledges the challenges they face, and focuses on proposing a theologically framed guide to planning as a way to embrace those opportunities. This book is then divided into four chapters and three postscripts—the previously noted four-fold approach. In a sequential manner, each of the four chapters weaves together lessons from Bonhoeffer's work with examples that inform the concluding questions.

Chapter 1, "Aspiration": The first chapter argues the ability of Christian colleges to meet the present challenges as opportunities as determined. The clarity with which they are defined by a model of Christian discipleship proves critical. This is a primary distinction of their very existence and a key attraction for students (and, in many cases, their parents, who are inextricably linked to their financial ability to attend). A sound discipleship model proves central in defining their aspirations. To this end, Bonhoeffer opens *Creation and Fall* by exploring what it means that "in the beginning God is."[26] The radical truth that comes from that exploration is that only God is God and that, in turn, human beings are not God. Any model of discipleship capable of informing how Christian colleges and universities navigate the anxious middle is defined first and foremost by that very acknowledgment. Doing so yields the freedom and, in turn, flourishing, which comes only from a life dependent upon God. The explorations of Monte

Cassino and L'Abri included in this chapter explore the clarity by which Christian colleges and universities articulate that understanding in their mission and purpose.

Questions that conclude this chapter include the following: What is the vision of discipleship animating a Christian college? In what way(s) is such an understanding of discipleship unique to a community that is both Christian and a college? How are members of the immediate Christian college community introduced to that understanding of discipleship? How are prospective members of a Christian college community introduced to that understanding of discipleship? What unique form of discipleship does it offer members of its community? Who is the audience for such an understanding of discipleship?

Chapter 2, "Imagination": Once a proper understanding of God is established as foundational to a model for Christian discipleship, the second chapter explores what it means for human beings to be created in God's image. Bonhoeffer is clear about the beauty of God's grace as it exists in the created order. Of God's creation, however, only humanity bears God's image. To this end, Bonhoeffer writes, "To say that in humankind God creates God's own image on earth means that humankind is like the Creator in that it is to be free. To be sure, it is free only through God's creation, through the word of God, it is free for the worship of the creator."[27] When rooted in this understanding, Christian colleges and universities find the true freedom to imagine what can become of the world around them because they inherit from God the ability to create, not something out of nothing as God did, but something out of something. As exemplified in a myriad of practices, cultivating that ability to imagine becomes the central function of the university. Examples included in this chapter detail the work of Brethren of Common Life and organizations such as the Council of Christian Colleges and Universities. Christian colleges and universities may not be fully embracing that potential, especially when that potential is not appropriated to its proper end.

Questions that conclude this chapter include the following: How does a Christian college cultivate the imagination of various members of its community? Among curricular educators? Cocurricular educators? Students? How is that imagination aligned with a particular vision of discipleship? How are members of the community encouraged to align their worship with their work? Being created in God's image, in what way is the imagination as exercised relational? Purposeful? Hopeful?

Chapter 3, "Collaboration": With the agency of a properly ordered imagination now in place, the third chapter turns to the question, with whom are we called to imagine and create? On this point, Bonhoeffer was clear, that we are meant to serve as cocreators not only with God but also with one another. The theological exegesis Bonhoeffer proposes in *Creation and Fall* allows us to understand ourselves as represented in Adam and Eve. As an extension of the relationship we share with God, Bonhoeffer calls us to view "the other wholly in the light of God's gift."[28] The divine mystery of humanity being created in God's image is based upon how "it actualizes to the highest possible degree [that Adam and Eve belong] to each other, which is precisely based upon their being different from one another."[29]

A properly ordered imagination is one that may begin alone but finds its highest expression this side of eternity in collaboration. Doing so allows for the diversity of gifts to be appreciated. The decisions Adam and Eve made in relation to the Tree of the Knowledge of Good and Evil, as Bonhoeffer contends, are not only decisions with which they struggled but decisions with which each person struggles daily. Collaboration cannot transcend that depravity, but it can serve as a means of acknowledging and confronting its limitations. Examples included in this chapter detail the historical legacy of cathedral schools and the ongoing impact of professional associations.

Questions that conclude this chapter include the following: What collaborative efforts do senior leaders of the Christian college model between their respective areas on campus? Between their respective areas and comparable areas on other campuses? In what way(s) is the Christian college organized (in terms of its intellectual and organizational architecture) to accomplish collaboration as a vision of discipleship? Are curricular units and programs aligned to facilitate collaboration? Are cocurricular units and programs aligned to facilitate collaboration? Are curricular and cocurricular programs and units aligned to facilitate collaboration? What reward structures, if any, encourage individuals and programs to work together? In what way(s) are educators on one campus encouraged to collaborate with educators on other campuses? What reward structures, if any, encourage such collaboration?

Chapter 4, "Illumination": The final chapter explores to what end Christian colleges and universities engage with the audiences they are called to serve. The depravity that plagues humanity and the collaboration defined by diverse gifts are highlighted by Bonhoeffer at the end of *Creation and Fall* and in the relationship shared by Cain and Abel. As with Adam and Eve and the decision they made at the Tree of the Knowledge of Good and Evil, the decisions that Cain and Abel made in relation to the gifts they produced and offered are not only decisions with which they struggled but decisions with which each person struggles each day. Cain and Abel were both called to prepare and share their gifts with the God they served. Cain and Abel, however, made different choices. While Abel's gift was a reflection of his desire to honor the Creator, Cain's gift was a reflection of his desire to honor himself. Bonhoeffer then writes, "Only the Creator can destroy life. Cain usurps for himself this ultimate right of the Creator and becomes the murderer [of Abel]."[30] The historical and contemporary examples included in this chapter explore the ways Christian colleges and universities honor their Creator through the ways they share the fruits of their labors. Examples included in this chapter detail the impact of the printing press and the University of Notre Dame's "What Would You Fight For?" series as well as its FaithND and ThinkND programs.

Questions that conclude this chapter include the following: Does the Christian college have a discernible messaging effort? If so, how is the messaging effort an extension of its understanding of discipleship? With what audience(s) is the Christian college poised to share that message? What messaging strategy coordinates such efforts? How are members of the community invited to participate in those efforts? What forms of professional development prepare those members to participate? When a crisis occurs, how is the Christian college prepared to respond? Respond as an extension of its understanding of discipleship? When that crisis passes, in what way(s) and with what speed does it return to its message?

Concluding Postscripts: The volume then closes with postscripts drafted by the presidents of three prominent colleges and universities that, each in its own way, sought since their respective foundings to be educational communities defined by the hope most concretely realized in the life, death, and resurrection of Jesus Christ. On a daily basis, these presidents grapple with the ways the histories and missions of their respective institutions are lived out amid the challenges and opportunities of the age in which we all live. As a result, their words at the end of this volume offer a sense of the complexities that come with such planning efforts.

The first postscript is offered by Jon S. Kulaga, who began his service in 2022 as the tenth president of Indiana Wesleyan University (IWU). Kulaga's thirty-four-year career in higher education includes a focus on leadership, strategic planning, advancement, and innovation, and a commitment to growing a Christ-centered university. Prior to his selection as president of IWU, Kulaga served as president of Ohio Christian University for five years, beginning in 2017. Kulaga has made notable achievements while serving in various executive and leadership roles, including chief academic officer and chief operating officer at Asbury University, and in academics, advancement, and student life development roles at Spring Arbor University. He was an ordained deacon and elder in the Free Methodist denomination for over thirty years before transferring his ordination to the Wesleyan denomination. He is an honorary Kentucky Colonel and has authored and contributed to six published books. He has presented and preached to students and churches in England, France, Haiti, Mexico, Japan, and China.

The second postscript is offered by Linda A. Livingstone, who began her service as president of Baylor University in 2017. During her undergraduate years at Oklahoma State University, Livingstone was also a member of the women's basketball team. She began her teaching and administrative career at Baylor but then, prior to returning as president, served as dean and professor of management at the Pepperdine University Graziadio Business School and dean and professor of management at the George Washington University School of Business. In addition to her duties at Baylor, Livingstone serves on a number of boards, including the American Council on Education's board of directors, the National Collegiate Athletic Association's (NCAA) Division I board of directors, and NCAA's board of governors.

The third postscript is offered by Beck A. Taylor, who began his service as president of Samford University in 2021. After working as an analyst for what is now Accenture, Taylor returned to Baylor as a faculty member and eventually served as associate dean for research and faculty development for the Baylor University Hankamer School of Business. He then served as dean and professor of economics for the Samford University Brock School of Business and as president of Whitworth University. In addition to publishing studies in a wide range of academic journals, Taylor's research has been referenced in publications including the *Boston Globe*, the *New York Times*, and the *Christian Science Monitor*.

* * *

What follows is not a manual for how Christian colleges and universities should navigate the anxious middle in which they currently find themselves. Such an effort, at best, could capture the particularity embodying one campus and, in turn, be of use only to that community. In contrast, what follows is a guide for how Christian colleges and universities should navigate the anxious middle.

Drawing from Dietrich Bonhoeffer's *Creation and Fall*, this guide is defined by the belief that a theologically informed understanding of discipleship is central to the efforts of any institution. Christian colleges and universities range greatly in terms of organizational type, geographic location, pedagogical delivery, and their relationship with a particular Christian tradition, to name only four. What follows is thus not only an argument for the importance of discipleship but also a guide that any institution or subentity within an institution can employ as it navigates the anxious middle in which it finds itself.

1

Aspiration

To close the 1932–1933 winter term, the text for the sermon Dietrich Bonhoeffer offered on Sunday, February 26, 1933, in Berlin's Trinity Church was Judges 6:15–16; 7:2; 8:23. Despite how we may remember Gideon, the army Gideon assembled, and the victories the Lord offered into that army's hands, Bonhoeffer opens by turning our expectations on their sides, if not upside down. In particular, he claims, "This is a passionate story about God's derision for all those who are fearful, and have little faith, all those who are much too careful, the worriers, all those who want to be somebody in the eyes of God but are not."[1] Comfort and security would not come by exercises of mere human effort. In Gideon, Bonhoeffer found a figure whose path to faith came when otherwise reasonable means were set aside.

To congregants living in World War I's wake of physical and existential deprivation, not to mention the recent rise of the Third Reich, one might expect Bonhoeffer to elevate Gideon as a heroic figure of the faith—a means of inspiration for an otherwise beleaguered people. In contrast, Bonhoeffer initially compounds the disorientation congregants must have felt on that Sunday when he confirmed Gideon's story as being "no rousing heroic legend—there is nothing of Siegfried in Gideon."[2]

19

Congregants gathered that morning would recognize Siegfried as an unconquerable hero found in Teutonic legends—legends to which Nazis were already turning as a means of swelling the nationalistic ego of a beleaguered people. In Gideon, Bonhoeffer wanted to vanquish any search for a conquering Christian hero, a hero in whom they could misplace their faith for deliverance.

The Germans whom Bonhoeffer addressed that morning were perhaps not that different from us. They believed in human potential, and they believed education was an important means of cultivating that potential. As a result, Germany became the educational and perhaps even cultural center of the Western world up to World War I. American scholars, for example, seeking what a singular focus on research could yield, made their way to Germany in the mid to late 1800s, returning to give life to universities such as Johns Hopkins and Chicago while also transforming some of the nation's oldest universities such as Harvard and eventually even Yale. The German research university was poised to shape the human mind in ways that would yield discoveries previously unimagined (and models that would prove the bane of many others wanting more emphasis on teaching and practical degrees).

Bonhoeffer believed that such efforts, when not rightfully ordered, were mere exercises of human will, exercises propelled by pride, exercises that ultimately resulted in destruction. The university, by its very nature, was formative and ordered people to particular ends, even if those ends were otherwise unarticulated or even unknown. In Judges 6:15; 7:2; 8:23, Bonhoeffer believes we witness God, however derisively, reminding Gideon that having "faith has the peculiar quality of always pointing away from the person's own self, toward the One in whose power, in whose captivity and bondage he or she is."[3]

As a result, Bonhoeffer's opening claim in this sermon is the same understanding that rests at the center of all understandings of discipleship—that only one altar exists to which human beings are to present themselves, "the altar of the Most High, the One and only, the Almighty, the Lord, to whom alone all creation bows down, before whom even the most powerful are but dust."[4] Only when such an understanding is in place can human beings truly understand their place in this world and to what end they are to labor. Bonhoeffer thus contends that human beings "are not heroes, not heroic, but rather creatures who are meant to do his will and obey him, whom he forces with mockery and love to be his servants."[5]

In this chapter, we contend that all efforts to plan for the future of a Christian college, to come to terms with what is possible at levels ranging from the institution-wide to the programmatic, must begin with clear conceptions of what it means for God to be God, for humans to be God's creation, and for humans to share in right relations with God—in the end, to be disciples. As noted in what follows, all practices—or, in this case, all educational practices—should orient humans toward a particular good or end to which they should aspire. No such endeavor is neutral in impact. In Bonhoeffer's estimation, the good to which humans should aspire is to obey God and do God's will. Everything else that follows in planning processes are just details.

A cursory review of recent plans developed by several Christian colleges and universities reveals that those conceptions—what it means for God to be God, for humans to be God's creation, and for humans to share in right relations with God—are often at best assumed. Christian colleges and universities rarely root their efforts in what it means for God to be God and for humans to be God's creation.[6] As a result, the details that follow in their plans fail to flow from clear understandings of discipleship and, in turn, are implicitly captive to a myriad of other narratives.

References to Jesus Christ may dot these documents, but such references often present as ornamentation designed to appeal to particular constituents. In the end, such appeasement allows for nothing more than the perpetuation of a Christian college, not its ability to thrive in the name of its Lord and Savior, Jesus Christ. When reviewing such plans, Bonhoeffer would likely note, "The Bible often speaks of God in heaven making fun of our human hustle and bustle, of God's laughter at the vain creatures he has made."[7]

* * *

In the beginning God created the heavens and the earth.
The earth was without form and void, and darkness was
upon the face of the deep; and the Spirit of God was mov-
ing over the face of the waters.

Genesis 1:1–2 (RSV)

In many ways, the sermon Bonhoeffer offered at Berlin's Trinity
Church on that morning was a summation of lectures he gave
over the course of the winter 1932–1933 semester. Inspired by
Karl Barth's determination to break with the historical-critical
efforts of the age, Bonhoeffer turned to Genesis 1–4:1 that
semester as a source for theological understanding concerning
how Christians could live at any point in time between Eden
and the Apocalypse, but, in particular, during what was proving
to be an anxious season. To their credit, the students who heard
Bonhoeffer offer those lectures that semester insisted he publish them. If they had not done so, we may never have known
what he offered during those unsettling days as the Third Reich
rose to power.

Central to what Bonhoeffer offered that semester and for
our focus on how Christian colleges can plan for the world
in which they find themselves is Bonhoeffer's opening claim:
"The church of Christ witnesses to the end of all things."[8] Such
a claim is eschatological in that it focuses our eyes on the end
of history and how one day all things will find their ultimate
fulfillment in Christ. As a result, the church "views the creation
from Christ; or better, in the fallen, old world it believes in the
world of the new creation, the new world of the beginning and
the end, because it believes in Christ and nothing else."[9] The
Church, and all other institutions to which she gives birth (such
as a Christian college), in turn, claim to serve in her name,
focus their sight by properly appreciating "the witness of Holy
Scripture."[10] Individuals draw inspiration from their study of
Scripture, but "the Bible is after all nothing other than the book

of the church."[11] As Christ's body, the Church bears witness to the end—that all things will find their fulfillment in Christ on the day of Christ's return.

While living in the anxious middle, that end informs how we understand God's abiding relationship with our predecessors, with us, and with those who may follow us. When understood properly, such an understanding does not provide a means of escape for the Church and a Christian college to which the Church gives birth; rather, it provides a means of understanding how to discern the paradoxical reality in which a Christian college finds itself—how to thrive in a world in which it ultimately does not belong.

As a result, Bonhoeffer contends that any reading of Genesis 1–4:1, a reading of the very beginning, must begin by understanding "the end of our whole world."[12] Debates concerning the historical and literary merits of Genesis 1–4:1 have their place. The story of creation, however, "must be read in a way that begins with Christ and only then moves to him as its goal."[13] Such a claim may not register as being radical in nature until one compares it to the state of biblical scholarship during Bonhoeffer's time and, in many ways, our own today. What currently presents as biblical scholarship, for example, is often captive to the competing stories of myriad individuals instead of being found in the magnanimous story of Jesus Christ—a story that knows its end, properly sees its beginning, and defines the present regardless of how great or small the challenges.

One way to assess the value of plans proposed by Christian colleges is to inquire about the size of the stories that animate them. Does that story, often more implicit than explicit yet nonetheless always present, reflect an appreciation for the end Christ alone ushers into existence? Or does that story reflect an appreciation for something smaller or, dare we say, petty? One way of discerning the difference between the two is by considering how much time is spent on such a plan or in meetings detailing the qualities that do not define an institution compared to detailing the qualities that do.

As discussed in the next chapter, the size of that story determines the size of an imagination. Small stories yield contradistinctive details. Large stories may eventually yield contradistinctive details but only as derivatives of distinctive details. The story Christ ushers into existence defines those distinctive details. Or, in the case of a Christian college, to what end should it aspire to order its efforts?

For example, a particular Christian college may be opposed to abortive practices. The primary issue at stake is not opposition to abortion but a commitment to God's gift of human life. A larger story calls Christians to be advocates for life in any number of circumstances, including circumstances in which the individual lives in question may be far less innocent than an unborn child. A smaller story will simply focus on opposition to a practice such as abortion. A commitment to life may compel Christians to oppose practices that compromise that commitment, including practices as disparate as capital punishment, warfare, and abortion. Failure to root convictions in the size of such a story leaves those convictions at risk of being captive to political predilection, not theological commitment.

When drawing upon *Creation and Fall* as a means of understanding to what end a Christian college should aspire to order its efforts, we propose that Bonhoeffer makes at least three points that merit consideration. First, while seemingly evident, Bonhoeffer challenges us to remember that God alone is God and that upon such an understanding all subsequent theological convictions find their proper place. "In the beginning—God" may be the most critical words in all of Scripture if for no other reason than no one could testify to the beginning other than God and God alone.

For Bonhoeffer, "God is the absolute beginning or the primal reality, who had being before our life and thinking, with all its anxiety. God alone tells us that God is in the beginning."[14] We can know of the beginning but by no means of our own. By various means of revelation, God testifies to the beginning, something that, again, God alone can do. Bonhoeffer would then go on to contend, "We can *know* of the beginning in the true sense only by hearing of the beginning while we ourselves are in the middle, between the beginning and the end."[15] Hearing, as we do in Scripture, is not the result of human speculation. By faith, hearing is an acceptance of the most fundamental condition of reality—God exists. God alone existed at the beginning, and what we know of God's existence is the result of God's revelation.

For Bonhoeffer, such a claim concerning God is not simply the result of ensuring that the most basic tenet of historic Christian orthodoxy be properly placed. Bonhoeffer would undoubtedly not overlook such details, but such details would not demand the lengths to which Bonhoeffer goes when noting that tenet at the outset of *Creation and Fall*. Perhaps doing so was necessary when addressing the congregation before him just as it might be for any Christian college at the outset of any planning process.

The underlying challenge is that communities charged with the cultivation of created potential often wrestle with the malady of practical atheism more than almost any other set of institutions to which the Church gives birth. Such a challenge lurks in questions we rarely pause to consider; nevertheless, it defines the pace of our days, the source of the talents we bear, or the truths we propose. Bonhoeffer belabors the points that God exists, that God alone existed at the beginning, and that what we know of God's existence is the result of God's creation as a means of confirming our radical dependence upon God. A properly ordered existence demands we never delude ourselves into thinking, however subtle the temptation, that we are God. Bonhoeffer would have nothing of such thinking in the winter of 1932–1933, nor should we as we navigate the anxious middle in which we currently find ourselves. The root conviction any Christian college must set before itself when planning for its future is that God exists.

Second, human beings, as with all creation, are God's creation. For Bonhoeffer, being God's creation demands we appreciate "that in the beginning God *created*."[16] As humans, we cannot step outside of ourselves—out of the middle in which we find ourselves—and in and by ourselves define the beginning. This beginning, the beginning in which God alone existed, "is distinguished by something utterly unique—unique not in the sense of a number that one can count back to, but in a qualitative sense, that is, in the sense that it simply cannot be repeated, that it is completely free."[17] All of creation, including the presence of humanity, is the result of God's nature as creator.

Part of what makes us as human beings unique among all of creation is our ability to reflect God's nature. Regardless, we are incapable of creating out of nothing. With God, Bonhoeffer argues, "There is simply nothing that provides [God with] the ground for creation. Creation comes out of this nothing. . . . God affirms the nothing only to the extent that God has already overcome it."[18] Humans create, but humans create out of something, the something that God created in its origin and to which proper appreciation is due.

For Bonhoeffer, this understanding is not simply affirmed in the opening words to Genesis but made possible to comprehend in full in the resurrection of Jesus Christ. Bonhoeffer goes so far as to offer that, absent a proper Christology, we cannot understand the full theological significance of God's ability to create out of nothing. To Bonhoeffer, "the dead Jesus Christ of Good Friday and the resurrected Lord of Easter Sunday [reflect] creation out of nothing, creation from the beginning."[19]

The nothingness out of which God created in the beginning is the same nothingness found on Holy Saturday, a void between Good Friday and Easter Sunday. Bonhoeffer goes so far as to argue, "There is absolutely no transition, no continuum between the dead Christ and the resurrected Christ, but the freedom of God that in the beginning created God's work out of nothing."[20] Failure to appreciate the theological significance of Christ's death and resurrection means humanity is incapable of appreciating what it means: "In the beginning—that is, out of freedom, out of nothing—God created heaven and earth."[21] Such an understanding proves critical to understanding how God relates to creation and thus serves as the foundation for how creation relates to God.

Third, only when we acknowledge that God alone is God and that God alone created out of nothing do we as human beings begin to understand what it means to be disciples—people who, by God's grace, participate in rightly ordered relationships with God and, in turn, with one another. In making this claim, Bonhoeffer confirms once again that "the creation still rests entirely in God's hands, in God's power; it has no being of its own."[22] Only then, however, can he go on to claim "the praise of the Creator is completed only when the creature receives its own being from God and praises God's being by its own being."[23]

In the first two verses of Genesis 1, Bonhoeffer sees the imprint of the relationship the Creator desired to have with creation and, in turn, what kind of relationship creation was called to share with the Creator. Apart from the Creator, creation has no being or even essence of its very existence. All that is present in creation is ultimately dependent upon the Creator. By the nature of its existence, creation is called to praise the Creator—such is its very purpose.

The relationship that creation and the Creator share, however, is not complete according to Bonhoeffer until it "praises God by its own being."[24] As asked and answered in the Westminster Shorter Catechism: "Q: What is the chief end of man? A: Man's chief end is to glorify God and to enjoy him forever." As with all creation, we find our being in God. Our being, however, finds its completion when we praise God as an expression of our own being.

The question then is, what role does a Christian college play in the lives of the individuals it serves? Is its chief end or aspiration, in whatever ways that aspiration may be exemplified, "to glorify God and to enjoy him forever"? Or do other aspirations, aspirations parading as distinctively Christian, define that aspiration? At the heart of any planning process, a Christian college is called by its very nature—or, borrowing from Bonhoeffer's terminology, *being*—to root its efforts in a clear understanding of discipleship whether the locale in which that understanding of discipleship is exercised is its library, laboratory, studio, recital hall, residence hall, or athletic field. Only when such an aspiration is clear and collectively embraced is the social imagination that gives life to a Christian college fully realized.

Aspiration Exemplified

When one of us crested the hill on a Judean wilderness excursion in 1977, he and a classmate startled a nun in the distance. She immediately scurried into the nearby monastery and closed its stalwart door. The classmate turned and said, "It's sad, the world will never touch them, and they will never touch the world."

Is that how people describe Christian colleges today? Although the classmate's declaration might be true of some monasteries and, for that matter, some modern colleges, we have options for better opportunities. The world is certainly touching (*and sometimes crushing*) religious colleges as a stream of new legislation poses threats to independence. Touching the world, however, is more in the colleges' control—though both aspects are inextricably linked.[25]

We will now pause to look at a historical example from the sixth century, a monastic movement where a clear operational mission meant everything—at a similar time to ours when this type of institution was threatened. We will do the same in the next section, with a modern example.

The commonplace use of *Benedictine* today is traced without any serious question to the *Rule of St. Benedict*—a simple seventy-three-chapter document (chapters ranging from a few sentences to a few manuscript pages).[26] Often simply referenced as *The Rule*, Benedict's effort led to the flourishing of the Western monastic movement. In recent years, Rod Dreher brought it much into the discussion of Christian institutions with his provocative best seller, *The Benedict Option: A Strategy for Christians in a Post-Christian Nation*.[27] In essence, he is calling for Christian institutions and leaders, like Benedict, to refocus on the core of Christianity (and acknowledge that in our current context it exhibits a distorted allegiance to a pervasive Moral Therapeutic Deism). The patron saint of Europe, Benedict of Nursia (d. ca. 548),[28] recognized the need for reform during the tumultuous sixth century.[29] (Yes, Dreher sees a similar decline in our culture and need for retreat, though not a total withdrawal.)[30] His remedy was order, influenced by John of Cassian (d. ca. 435). Such an understanding of order of schedules and routines came with the larger purpose of predisposing his fellow monks into a mind of worship and spiritual awareness. The need for stability and obedience permeates his *Rule*, though his list of rules was actually much more relaxed than previous arrangements. Diarmaid MacCulloch, emeritus professor of history of the Church (Oxford), states, "His changes breathe the simplicity, a sense of terse style, and a gentler, less autocratic attitude than the Master [*Regula Magistri*] to the community which an abbot must lead."[31] The *Rule* included two cooked meals, wine, bedding, poverty but shared possessions, and a manner for discussion of differences—all relaxed changes compared to the older master (early sixth century).

To ensure stability, Benedict built into the *Rule* a lifetime commitment to the community that adherents joined, which "proved one of the sources of the institution's great relevance in a time of chaos."[32] It also helped counter the proliferation of wandering monks and thwarted what the early church's *Didache* addressed—parasitic pastors (or preachers of various sorts). A "novelty" of the *Rule* when compared to earlier guidelines (like the *Regula Magistri*) "is that every monk is considered responsible for the entire community."[33] It is a bit mind-boggling to think of such a rule; keep in mind, this was a new injunction. It would be like today asking professors or administrators within a denomination to do the same at their religious institutions: to commit to one institution for life (unless asked by the modern equivalent of their abbot—a denominational leader[s]—to change colleges).

To ensure obedience, Benedict built in a rather regimented day and a willingness to follow the formative and summative guidance of their father figure, the abbot. His mission was manifest in not only the rule itself but the ramifications of building intercommunity connections. Yes, part of this was his top-down administrative brilliance. Concomitantly, it was the bottom-up understanding of what was being implemented, and why. The adage proved true for the participants—if the why is big enough, the how will show up.

Benedict founded at least a dozen communities (twelve monks around an abbot) and was the founder of the first Benedictine abbey at majestic Monte Cassino, but it is his *Rule* that outlived him. Cassino itself was sacked, destroyed, and abandoned several times—and was even the site of the Battle of Monte Cassino during World War II as a Nazi stronghold (in 1944 the Allied forces bombed it into surrender). The inhumane agenda of the Nazis cost nearly eighty thousand lives during those four months alone, mainly to the Allied forces. The irony is that the monastery where the *Rule* was founded and became the launching point for a type of holy community in the region also became the stopping point for an unholy one. Today, about a dozen monks serve at the abbey at Monte Cassino and enjoy the gorgeous confines of the new structure rebuilt by the state. The current abbot is the 192nd in the continuum from St. Benedict.

Many aspects of the *Rule* are commonplace among our religious nomenclature—not least are the prayer hours: matins, lauds, prime, terce, sext, none, vespers, and compline. Although the rationales for the various lists of hours and special dates vary among the branches of Christianity and are beyond our study here, the beginnings can be traced to Psalm 119:164 (RSV): "Seven times a day I praise thee for thy righteous ordinances." The third, sixth, and ninth hours (terce, sext, and none) are associated with Christ's passion. Since the Second Vatican Council, the three major hours are matins, lauds, and vespers.[34]

With these came a considerable impact on those outside their walls through the breviaries[35] and the abbreviated *Book of Hours*. The latter became the most common printed source to survive the Middle Ages. These manuscript codices and later printed books, designed to help laity follow readings for these hours, were often made by the monks. More Bibles were needed as services around these prayer times (also called "offices" from the official times) added music and Scripture readings, psalters, hymnals, and lectionaries.

The monks' balanced life positioned work as part of a pre-scribed form of worship. This same work component would factor into the monasteries' economic well-being through farming and other industries. We find a bit of this today in work colleges like Berea and College of the Ozarks.

Using their intellect, especially for the gifted, became many monks' main work—that of scholarship. "The shade of Jerome, who had taken so much trouble to shape that thought, would be gratified, and otherwise the story of Western Europe would have been very different."[36] Jerome had argued that study and writing "were as demanding, difficult and heroically self-denying as any physical extravagance" of monks, including those especially near him in Syria and those in Egypt.[37]

The *Rule* reflected Benedict's aspiration for holy living, especially in a community of monks. It proved so clear that it reaches into the present. At least twenty Benedictine colleges were founded in the United States alone, with the largest being Benedictine University in Lisle, Illinois (some seven thousand students). What surfaces as well in rather diverse places is the operational guidelines for a major database management engine, SQLite—"used in most major browsers, smart phones, Adobe products, and Skype."[38] Founder D. Richard Hipp based this on the *Rule*'s main section, chapter 4 (the seventy-three "tools for good works"). SQLite's instruction manual reads: "This code of ethics has proven its mettle in thousands of diverse communities for over 1,500 years, and has served as a baseline for many civil law codes since the time of Charlemagne."[39] This seems to counter Dreher's *Benedict Option*.

We find in the *Rule* a response built squarely around a radical mission with clear guidelines—one built on past rulebooks and one that discarded operational objects that impeded both survival and missional success. Such an aspiration writ large led to financial stability and a mission that fueled partnerships beyond or without walls, with some shared governance but independence (perhaps not unlike the CCCU, International Alliance for Christian Education [IACE], National Association of Independent Colleges and Universities [NAICU], and others). If we can use the following as an operational definition for *institution*, then we find with Benedict the power of mission to build such systems. In the end, an institution is a systematic response to a recurring need. The key is to identify the need solidly within a vibrant biblical orthodoxy.

Some 1,400 years after Benedict founded Monte Cassino, other Christian leaders started an educational ministry in the mountains, away from "the relentlessly secular culture" of the twentieth century. In 1955, Edith and Francis Schaeffer began L'Abri in their Swiss chalet southeast of Lake Geneva. Its name is French for "shelter" and puts one in mind of Dreher's *Benedict Option*.

In a sense, L'Abri represents Dreher's cause for pause from the cascading cultural pressures. However, instead of orthodox Christians retreating to form a plan with answers, L'Abri became (and is) a shelter where people seek truth while identifying and engaging in life's main philosophical questions. In the end, as the Schaeffers postulated, it will help visitors to leave with a better understanding of God's sovereignty over all of life.[40]

Miroslav Volf agrees with this intentional religious approach in his counter to the thesis of *Education's End*, written by another Yale professor, Anthony Kronman. Volf rejects Kronman's default "sacrifice of intellect" among religious educators. "As a person of faith," argues Volf, "I think that a secular quest for the meaning of life is very likely to fail, and that the viable candidates for the meaning of life are all religiously based."[41] L'Abri was founded as such a place, for such a foundation, and birthed such a movement.

L'Abri's approach (framed within the German notion of a "worldview") was not merely to reflect on culture but to engage it. A litany of "Christian transformation educators" have inspired waves of students through clear core tenets of their messages and/or systems to sustain such teachings. The authors of this book were colleagues (and one a former student) of such an educator, the late Glenn Martin. He was the regular keynoter for Youth with a Mission seminars (via University of the Nations) on "the biblical Christian worldview." The mission and clarity of his teaching to hundreds of students, including many from other countries, to the remote campus of Indiana Wesleyan University (then the tiny Marion College) proved instrumental. In a sense, his worldview mantra was the fulcrum of his in-house L'Abri—Marion's history and political science department. His lectures at Wheaton and then at IWU predated and then overlapped with Schaeffer's prolific years—whose resources Martin required of his majors.

For those familiar with the L'Abri narrative, it is difficult to separate the community and movement from the intensity and transformational teaching of Francis Schaeffer (in person and via his resources). This dynamic played out throughout history with teachers such as Abelard (1079–1142) and today with those like Eric Cunningham at Gonzaga University (also a professor of history). He is laser-focused from each semester's inaugural lecture and unabashed about his intentions: "Because I want all students to follow the way of the Lord, I work hard to show them that nothing is neutral. All of life is religious. Believing that the whole world belongs to God and will ultimately give allegiance to God . . . I want students to see that God wants all areas of culture to be redeemed."[42]

Andy Crouch shows an appreciation for this approach and particularly Schaeffer in *Culture Making: Recovering Our Creative Calling* (2008). He surmises that Schaeffer championed to "engage" culture, "a term that would become a watchword for a whole evangelical generation."[43] The "dominant posture" at L'Abri, he argues, was to analyze culture, "often impressively nuanced and learned analysis, to be sure." Through Crouch's lenses, however brilliant the L'Abri founders' teaching and approach, enacting such views once students left the community proved difficult. "It is perhaps not unfair to say that to this day, evangelicalism, so deeply influenced by the Schaeffers [Francis and his wife, Edith] and their many protégés, still produces better art critics than artists."[44]

We find a glimpse of this intense post-L'Abri reflection in many writers, including Steven Garber: "In many ways the intellectual world I began to explore in those months is the one I am still exploring more than twenty years later; it gave me questions and categories sufficiently complex that I have not yet come to their end.... The L'Abri folk set me on a course of seeing the connection between presuppositions and practice."[45] However, the very book quoted here, Garber's *Fabric of Faithfulness*, demonstrates quite a stride from reflection to engagement, as it helped countless students navigate "the critical years," during which they find ways to put their beliefs into action in the world in which they live.

Francis died in 1984,[46] and Edith in 2013, but their ministry lives on via L'Abri International Communities. These "are study centers where individuals have the opportunity to seek answers to honest questions about God and the significance of human life. L'Abri believes that Christianity speaks to all aspects of life."[47]

The L'Abri communities (including both study and resource centers) are in some ten countries and have inspired a mélange of other movements. They collectively celebrated the movement's fifty-year anniversary in 2004, with more than a thousand attendees at their celebration in St. Louis, Missouri, with speakers of the ilk of Os Guinness and Charles Colson.[48]

Reminiscent of the "community" aspect of the Benedictines, God is considered "over all of life"—perhaps Francis Schaeffer's mantra. Members of these communities are nearly always short term; their stays range from a couple of weeks to a few months. Though the emphasis throughout is on seeking truth and studying in the wake of Schaeffer's presuppositional analysis, a hands-on work component is also involved.

Dreher acknowledges L'Abri in his discussion of the Christian Study Center movement, which began in 1968 at the University of Virginia. "Inspired by L'Abri Fellowship, the international network of Evangelical study centers founded by Francis and Edith Schaeffer, the Charlottesville group eventually bought a house on Chancellor Street near campus and set up headquarters. . . . The center takes applying Christian discipleship to the life of the mind seriously, and it shows."[49] And indeed, the movement continues to grow, with thirty-four study centers in the United States and Canada, now linked through a consortium.[50]

The consortium's description of its campus gathering spaces and aspirations are a blend of Benedict of Nursia's intentionality—a clear and simple mission, Dreher's "Benedict Option" or a cause to pause to think seriously about Christians in culture, and a modified retreat from normal traffic. The houses provide such:

> Christian Study Centers are communities of students and scholars animated by the ancient ideal of *faith seeking understanding*. Located adjacent to colleges and universities, study centers support and complement their host institution's mission to discover and disseminate knowledge by convening conversations that address the big questions of life—questions of meaning, purpose and value. In addition to public lectures, many study centers offer intimate conversations and comfortable hospitality in their own facilities.[51]

The main difference from the *Rule* is that these communities vary widely in rules, if any at all (besides gathering as Christians and endorsing the Apostles' Creed). The consortium's stated mission is more college focused than L'Abri. Both communities prepare students for reentering the world (as if they actually ever leave it), whereas Benedict was preoccupied with spiritual growth and love for a stable community (and lifelong residence). At the Rivendell Institute at Yale University, founded by one of the pioneers of the consortium, David Mahan, a key part of the institute's mission is "examining the state of the contemporary university and formulating Christian responses to all areas of academic inquiry."[52] Another key part, also addressed by Mahan, is to counter the evangelistically successful but perhaps institutionally disconnected efforts of major historic parachurch organizations. The consortium's stated mission is: "To catalyze and empower thoughtful Christian presence and practice at colleges and universities around the world, in service of the common good."[53]

From L'Abri to the consortium of study centers, we find clues of a stickiness of a tight mission, of aspiration—one that also has in its recipe ingredients that attract students and loyal patrons. Like Benedict, there is the ingredient of dedicated space—whether a remote chalet, a dedicated campus center or building, or a departmental office complex and classrooms. There is also the ingredient of ultimate questions (and supporting texts). In all of these examples, leaders (professors or otherwise) become a key ingredient. But overall, Volf's candidness tips the scales of the weightiest ingredient—the spiritual beginning and ending of it all. This candidness, this robust and unabashed declaration to the pursuit of knowledge and cultural engagement through a Christian lens, proves critical, as Schaeffer, Martin, and many others espouse.

Like Monte Cassino and L'Abri, Christian colleges have the ability and imperative to recruit key thinkers (and develop future ones). There is a magnetism, the fuel for a movement with enrollment consequences, for thoughtful and overtly Christian responses to questions from outside their walls, and from the other side of Zoom screens.

Aspiration Explored

Drawing from Bonhoeffer's reading of the first two verses in Genesis and the examples offered by the *Rule of Saint Benedict* and the L'Abri, we contend clarity of aspiration is the most fundamental component of any planning process, whether that process be undertaken at the programmatic level or the institutional level.

Furthermore, in Bonhoeffer, St. Benedict, and Francis Schaeffer, we find that any expression of community the Church may bring to life is, at its core, an expression of Christian discipleship. A social service agency, hospital, retirement home, and Christian college all implicitly or explicitly express such an understanding. The question we ask a Christian college to pose to itself at the outset of any planning process is this: What understanding of discipleship informs its aspirations? To help foster such a conversation, we propose grappling with the following questions.

- *First, what is the vision of discipleship animating a Christian college?*

This question should generate a common sense of awareness among all individuals invested in a particular planning process of the vision for discipleship that defines their community and/or subcommunity. One would hope that such an understanding is delineated at an institution-wide level in publications, such as student and employee handbooks, that then inform conversations and decisions all the way down to the programmatic level. As we posed may be the case, a Christian college may not have grappled with the basic question, what form of discipleship animates this school's existence? If that is the case, looking at this foundational issue before advancing to the next step in the planning process will prove beneficial. Even if a unified understanding of discipleship exists, we would join with Bonhoeffer, St. Benedict, and Francis Schaeffer in contending that an assessment of the theological adequacy of such an understanding still needs to be conducted. In essence, a Christian college should ask: How well does it delineate what it means for God to be God, for humans to be God's creation, and for humans to be in right relations with God? Some revision may prove necessary. Or some revision may prove necessary as a result of threats to that understanding that are circulating in the wider culture.

- *Second, in what way(s) is such an understanding of discipleship unique to a community that is both Christian and a college?*

Being able to specify in theologically robust detail what it means for God to be God, for humans to be God's creation, and for humans to be in right relations with God ensures that the aspirations for discipleship are Christian. Doing so does not ensure that such aspirations are properly focused for a Christian college. The Church may give life to a Christian college, but a Christian college is not the Church. As a result, an understanding of discipleship that is contextually appropriate for the Church's aspirations is not contextually appropriate for the aspirations of a Christian college. Such an assertion does not mean such understandings are mutually exclusive of each other but rather reflective of the relationship they share as distinct institutions. The Church gives birth to a Christian college as a community that "take[s] every thought captive to obey Christ,"[54] only then to be shared with members of the next generation along with whatever public a Christian college is called to serve.

- *Third, how are members of the immediate Christian college community introduced to that understanding of discipleship?*

In the most general possible terms, members of the immediate Christian college community fall into two groups—students and employees. Both groups participate in a common aspiration of discipleship even if they do so in a myriad of ways. Students, whether undergraduates or graduates, enroll at a Christian college for a season and do so generally with the intention of earning a degree. Although students participate in practices determined by employees, some of the most formative exercises they experience are facilitated by other students. Some of those experiences are formal and sanctioned by the university; some are informal. The question concerning students then is, how are they introduced to the school's understanding of discipleship? Is that introduction formal and/or informal? Assuming that introduction is offered by a myriad of sources, does that introduction reflect a unifying depth of appreciation? Or is that introduction fragmented and perhaps even conflicted?

These days, few employees—whether staff members, faculty members, and/or administrators—serve a particular Christian college for the entirety of their professional careers. Regardless of the duration of their service, they bring with them impressions of discipleship they obtained from educational institutions they attended as well as institutions where they previously served. Although such diversity of institutional backgrounds greatly adds to the ability of a particular Christian college to take all thought captive, it also poses the question concerning how an appreciation for the understanding of discipleship is fostered. As with students, does that communication reflect a unifying depth of appreciation? Or is that communication fragmented and perhaps conflicted?

- *Fourth, how are prospective members of a Christian college community introduced to that understanding of discipleship?*

Long before prospective members of a Christian college community become students or employees, impressions of discipleship mount as a result of their experience with messaging received via the institution's website, social media platforms, and publications. As a result, the answer to this question builds with each successive point of contact prior to encountering, in the case of students, an admissions officer, or, in the case of employees, a human resources officer. As was previously asked, does that communication reflect a unifying depth of appreciation? Or is that communication fragmented and perhaps conflicted? Ideally, students and employees should have a clear understanding of who they individually and collectively can become by the time they decide whether to join the community.

- *Fifth, how are guests of a Christian college community introduced to that understanding of discipleship?*

Guests may have no interest in becoming members of a Christian college community. Regardless, they can make valued contributions to the community while also benefiting from that community, however short the duration of their visit.

In the fragmented age in which we live, some of the most vigorous debates that occur on college and university campuses unfortunately focus on criteria employed when deciding whether to invite a particular speaker to campus. We are eager to witness the dawning of an age in higher education in which discussion and debate among reasonable, substantive, and charitable people, regardless of whether they agree or disagree, is not only encouraged but viewed as being of great value. For a Christian college, one of our theories is that the greater the sense of appreciation an institution has for its understanding of discipleship, the greater its eagerness to serve as a venue for such expressions of discussion and debate. In essence, an understanding of discipleship fosters the hope needed to view such experiences as opportunities, not threats.

A great number of guests to whom a Christian college may extend invitations are likely individuals who represent their understanding of discipleship in ways that can inform and inspire members of the college community. When evaluating whether to extend invitations to guests who may not represent a Christian college's understanding of discipleship, community members will have a clear rationale for doing so and consider how even a voice to the contrary can strengthen such an understanding.

Even prior to considering an invitation, guests should be introduced to an understanding of the discipleship that animates a Christian college. Only then can a guest decide how to evaluate an invitation. If a guest accepts an invitation, a guest can then understand how to reach out to and interact with audience members. In the case where a guest declines, a guest can have access to the information needed to inform a reasonable rationale for doing so.

* * *

Regardless of whether the planning process is designed to represent the hopes of a particular program or the institution as a whole, the questions at the outset of the process are the same: What does it mean for God to be God, for humans to be God's creation, and for humans to share in right relations with God?

The answers to those questions unveil the sufficiency or insufficiency of inspiration animating a Christian college—in essence, how discipleship is understood. Insufficiency in whatever form it manifests itself is first and foremost detrimental to the relationship members of a Christian college community share with God and with one another. Insufficiency in whatever form it manifests itself, however, is also detrimental for a Christian college fulfilling its calling as a Christian college.[55]

All too often, insufficient understandings of discipleship lead to insufficient exercises of imagination when it comes to discerning what a Christian college is called to achieve. Such pressures come in at least two forms. First, sentimentality allows mediocrity to parade as excellence. In essence, individuals resist confronting colleagues about subpar work due to fear of hurting feelings.[56] Regardless of how true such feedback might be, culture dictates that no greater sin can be committed than being perceived as mean. As a result, excellence proves indistinguishable from the lowest common denominator.

Second, "hell hath no fury greater than the second-rate."[57] All too often, achievements that rise to levels of distinction are mocked for being products of arrogance and/or the appropriation of time and energy on culturally unworthy tasks. The argument that a Christian college is a teaching institution, for example, makes such thinking recognizable. At its best, it explicitly points to a commitment to teaching. At its worst, it implicitly justifies a lack of commitment to research.[58] In such a culture, faculty members who publish learn to hide or, when discovered, downplay the fruits of their labors.

In contrast, a sufficient understanding of discipleship is rooted in the cost that Christ paid for our salvation—a price too high for mediocrity to be viewed as a sufficient response. What a Christian college imagines as excellence is an exercise of gratitude—a matter to which we will now turn our attention.

2

Imagination

At the close of the 1932–1933 winter term, Dietrich Bon-hoeffer knew the greatest question he and the congregants who joined him on that Sunday in Berlin's Trinity Church were facing was the depth of their theological imagination in the face of mounting challenges.

In a letter to the American theologian Reinhold Niebuhr, dated February 6, 1933, Bonhoeffer states, "The path ahead for the church has seldom looked so gloomy."[1] In a letter dated April 14, 1933, to Erwin Sutz, the Swiss minister who introduced Bonhoeffer to Karl Barth, Bonhoeffer acknowledges the need to "rescue the church." In particular, he presses, "The Jewish question is also giving the church a great deal of trouble, and here the most intelligent people have totally lost their heads and their Bible."[2]

Bonhoeffer, perhaps better than almost anyone else in recent history, knew the response to the challenges the Church was facing was one fostered not by a fearful, near-sighted imagination but by a hopeful search for a home in which the Church truly belonged.[3]

Despite how Gideon struggled to adjust his sight to such an imagination, in Judges 6:15–16; 7:2; 8:23, Bonhoeffer finds in Gideon someone who experienced God's call in a way that would benefit the Church during the anxious season they were experiencing. The Nazis and the responses they were beginning to issue to "the Jewish question" were metaphorically comparable to what Gideon faced when surveying the Midianites—"an enemy nation with superior power."[4]

Bonhoeffer notes that Gideon's imagination was initially captured by his assessment of the disparities he witnessed: "He looks at himself and his own strength and then at the unconquerable might of the opposing side. He has nothing on his side—the enemy has it all."[5] In that moment, Bonhoeffer acknowledges that Gideon realized he and the Israelites, on their own, were outnumbered. Bonhoeffer also offers, "Gideon is someone we know, isn't he? He has suddenly become very much alive for us. Gideon, we recognize your voice only too well; you sound the same today as you did then."[6]

In that sense, Bonhoeffer also recognizes that the Church's imagination can go one way or another. An understandably fearful imagination would look at the might of the Nazis, the evil they represent, and accommodate—just as greater numbers of Bonhoeffer's brethren were beginning to do so. If survival, and in particular survival by human might, was what defined their fearful imagination, such accommodation was not only reasonable but also perhaps even prudent. If what defined their imagination was rooted in an understanding of discipleship defined by a world in which they would belong one day, then hope in something far greater than human might proves necessary.

At this point, Bonhoeffer resorts to pointing out how God, again however derisively, reminded Gideon of the size of the imagination that should define what was possible. Gideon wanted to know with what army was he supposed to defeat such an enemy. Yet the Lord, in Bonhoeffer's estimation, responded to Gideon, and at that moment in Germany, by saying in effect, "Shut up. You're asking, 'With what?' Haven't you realized what it means that this God is calling to you? Isn't the call of God enough for you; if you listen properly, doesn't it drown out all your 'with what' questions?"[7]

In Bonhoeffer's estimation, Gideon's imagination and the imagination of the congregants gathered on that day were to be defined by God's hopeful assertion, "'I will be with you'—that means you are not asked to do this with any other help. 'It is I who have called you; I will be with you; I shall be doing it too.'"[8] We would argue that Bonhoeffer poses a question to Gideon, to the congregation gathered on that day, and to us today: "Do you hear that, Gideon of yesterday and today? God has called you, and that is enough."[9]

Most of us likely remember how God then expanded Gideon's imagination and how Gideon learned that God was—is—enough. However insufficient Gideon's original army was in comparison to the army of the Midianites, God redirected Gideon's attention, asking him to "look at this army of yours; it's too big."[10] Theologically the problem is not so much with the literal size of the army but with the imagination Gideon exercised when estimating what he might need when wading into battle with the army before him. At this juncture, Bonhoeffer proposes that God asks, "Gideon, where is your faith? Look at this army of yours; it's too big; Gideon; it was fear and doubt that made you call up this army."[11] However insufficient the physical stature of the army Gideon called, that army was still the mightiest army he could summon. Fear informed his imagination to match human might with human might the best he could.

Bonhoeffer then notes that the only way God could expand Gideon's imagination, to reorient it from fear to hope, was to tell Gideon to send his army—however insufficient its size—home. At this point, Bonhoeffer, to the congregants before him on that day in Berlin, once again points out the derisive nature of God's interaction with Gideon. Bonhoeffer even goes so far as to label God's demand as a "phenomenal" and "a confusing encounter with the living God!"[12] Detailing such an encounter, Bonhoeffer writes:

> There stands Gideon with his little army, hesitating to go out against the enemy's superior forces, and then God comes and laughs rudely in his face, makes fun of him: "Gideon,

the troops with you are too many for me." Instead of bringing on huge amounts of weapons and armies, he calls for disarmament, meaning faith; let your armies go home![13]

Only when stripped of everything in which he could falsely invest his confidence could Gideon's imagination be oriented toward the hope that only faith in God could afford.

Bonhoeffer's larger point, the point he wanted his congregants to hear, was whether they were willing to let their armies go home—whether they would recognize that the Germany in which they lived was also not a Germany in which they belonged. The Nazis took power that winter, their storm troopers were growing in number, and the "Jewish question" was dividing the Church. Bonhoeffer believed that because God created humans in God's image, human aspirations were defined by their understanding of discipleship. Only such aspirations could properly order the imagination to the hope that Christ alone makes possible. The Nazis may be growing in power, and their power may seem insurmountable. With Gideon at his side, Bonhoeffer implores not only his congregants on that morning but also all of us who have ears to hear to "fall down before [our] God and let God be [our] Lord; know that only God can save [us]."[14]

* * *

Then God said, "Let us make man in our image, after our likeness; and let them have dominion over the fish of the sea, and over the birds of the air, and over the cattle, and over all the earth, and over every creeping thing that creeps upon the earth." So God created man in his own image, in the image of God he created him; male and female he created them.

—Genesis 1:26–27 (RSV)

When properly rooted in an understanding of discipleship, a Christian college is well-positioned to exercise a hopeful imagination in whatever strategic planning processes—processes from the programmatic to institution wide—may follow. Although a number of recent institution-wide planning processes are reflective of the exercise of hopeful imagination, others are rooted in fear and inherently small in terms of what they reflect God has called them to accomplish. With that temptation in mind, the University of Notre Dame's president, John I. Jenkins, C.S.C., closed his inaugural address on September 23, 2005, with the admonishment, "Let no one ever again say that we dreamed too small."[15]

One way to discern an inherently small plan is to ask whether its goals are goals almost any other institution would embrace. For example, although few would argue against increasing public engagement on the part of the faculty, does such a goal come with details concerning to what end or for what purpose a Christian college should increase public engagement? Few would argue against increasing the emotional health of the student body. The question to ask, however, is whether such a goal comes with details concerning to what end the emotional health of a Christian college's student body is being increased. A hopeful imagination, an imagination rooted in an aspiration of discipleship, allows a plan to propose goals that may otherwise seem impossible or, to others who lack such an imagination, nonsensible.

In Gideon, in the congregants gathered that morning, and dare we say in us, Bonhoeffer recognizes people whom God created in God's image. As argued in the previous chapter, Bonhoeffer's *Creation and Fall* provides an apt theological backdrop to appreciate in full what Bonhoeffer was proposing on that day in Berlin about the relationship Gideon shared with God and the relationship we all share with God. As a whole, the creation narrative is an account of the relationship God yearns to be in with God's creation.

For our purposes, Genesis 1:26–27 is among the most profound biblical passages in terms of understanding not only that relationship but also how such a relationship is rooted in what it means to be human. Being created in God's likeness, humanity, while not God, is endowed with qualities of God's image. Those very qualities lead God to charge humanity with the responsibility of having dominion over all other created beings—beings prized by God but not created in God's image. A properly exercised imagination is one of the greatest ways humanity reflects what it means to be in God's image. To fully appreciate such an understanding and how it defines the imagination, at least three lessons need to be drawn from Bonhoeffer's exploration of Genesis 1:26–27 in *Creation and Fall*.

First, Bonhoeffer argues that human beings were created by a God who creates freely and that the ability to create freely is one of God's definitive qualities. For Bonhoeffer, "if the Creator wishes to create the Creator's own image, then the Creator must create it free. And only such an image, in its freedom, would fully praise God, would fully proclaim God's glory as Creator."[16] Underlying this assumption by Bonhoeffer is the understanding that (1) God is free and (2) that characteristic is essential to God's identity. As beings created in God's image, human beings must, in turn, also bear that characteristic and be free. Although human beings bear God's image, as Bonhoeffer notes from the very beginning of *Creation and Fall*, human beings are not God. Human beings may exercise that freedom in ways that curve away from themselves, toward God, and toward the rest of creation. However, human beings may also exercise freedom in ways that curve in on themselves, away from God, and away from the rest of creation.

As Bonhoeffer contends, human beings are capable of fully praising God and fully proclaiming God's glory when they exercise their freedom in ways that curve away from themselves. By virtue of what it means to offer such a response and do so fully, human beings must be free. Praising God and proclaiming God's glory must be a free response by the created being to its Creator. Even though Scripture offers such a record of humanity's creation, Bonhoeffer also argues that we human beings can never fully understand our identity in our original state. In fact, Bonhoeffer goes so far as to say that doing so is hopeless, his reasoning being that "it fails to recognize that it is only from Christ that we can know about the original nature of humankind."[17] That recognition leads us back to Bonhoeffer's emphasis on discipleship and our argument that an understanding of discipleship is fundamental to a Christian college and any planning process it initiates.

Second, Bonhoeffer then turns his attention to how freedom, as definitive of the Creator and the relationship the creature shares with the Creator, is understood. As previously noted, *Creation and Fall* was originally delivered as a set of lectures in the winter of 1932 and 1933 at the University of Berlin. Bonhoeffer's audience for those lectures, as is also true for us, was socially conditioned to think of freedom as being an individual capacity. The fundamental social unit, in essence, that determined the context in which freedom was exercised was the singular, autonomous individual.

Bonhoeffer, however, turns that understanding on its side by arguing, "Freedom is a relation between two persons. Being free means 'being-free-for-the-other,' because I am bound to the other. Only by being in relation with the other am I free." Bonhoeffer then continues to challenge contemporary perceptions by contending that freedom "is not an ability, a capacity, [or] an attribute of being." Freedom is something that resides not within an individual but between individuals. Freedom is "simply something that comes to happen, that takes place, that happens to me through the other."[18]

Bonhoeffer's argument concerning freedom is ultimately rooted, however, in the relationship that God shares with persons of the Trinity and that God chooses to share with humanity. Being created in God's image and "likeness" is not an analogy of being or an *analogia entis* as a couple of Bonhoeffer's contemporaries proposed.[19] In contrast, Bonhoeffer believes, "Analogia relatonis is therefore the relation which God has established, and it is analogia in this relation which God has established."[20]

Finally, Bonhoeffer challenges not only the nature of freedom but the end to which freedom is exercised. Bonhoeffer's contemporaries, as with the majority of us, likely think of freedom at best by an absence of restraints. As a result, freedom knows of no particular end or purpose except for the fact that individuals may choose how to exercise it entirely on their own and within the contexts populated by the widest array of unencumbered possibilities. Some of the most vexing moral and legal questions in the West emerge when such possibilities seem encumbered.[21]

In contrast to freedom being best exercised in contexts populated by the widest array of unencumbered possibilities, Bonhoeffer presses, "There is no 'being-free-from' without 'being-free-for.'"[22] Freedom, by its very nature, is defined by an end or a purpose. Only when that end or purpose is clear do discussions about what encumbrances prove sensible rise above arbitrary inclinations otherwise parading as political or social logic. Bonhoeffer thus pleads, "There is no dominion without serving God; in losing the one humankind necessarily loses the other." As a result, "human freedom for God and the other person and human freedom from the creature in dominion over it constitute the first human beings' likeness to God."[23] As Bonhoeffer's own life would exemplify, such an understanding not only yields what encumbrances to freedom are worthy of resistance; it also yields when such resistance is worthy even of giving one's life.

Rooted in what it means to be created in God's image, the imagination Bonhoeffer offers is relational, purposeful, and hopeful. Rooted in its aspiration for discipleship, a Christian college is well-served by prayerfully leveraging this form of imagination to its greatest extent in the planning process.

To be clear, such a form of imagination is not the product of whimsical daydreaming. In addition, such a form of imagination refuses to be captured by conventional thinking that parades as wisdom. Such an imagination seeks to bear all that God may be calling a community—ranging from the programmatic to the institution wide—to pursue. Creighton University president Daniel S. Hendrickson, S.J., defined such an imagination as "the way people envision a social existence with one another. It includes the ways by which people envision or imagine the combined reality of a sense of self and ways of engaging the world."[24]

For a Christian college, that engagement may mean sending home one's army, to use the Gideon story as metaphor. Then again, that engagement may mean calling up an army greater than one ever envisioned. The question is not the size. The question is about whether the understanding that defines it is the product of an imagination rooted in an aspiration of discipleship.

Imagination Exemplified

Imagine hearing of a cluster of leading Christian thought leaders who share an educational journey. A radical upstart program grew out of such a context in the Middle Ages around the Sisters and Brethren of the Common Life. Though its adherents eventually filled monasteries, individuals passing through its hospices and schools included luminaries the ilk of Nicholas of Cusa (key proponent of Renaissance humanism), Thomas à Kempis (author of *The Imitation of Christ*), and Desiderius Erasmus (often labeled "the morning star of the Reformation").[25]

The first three were all part of the same fraternity in east-central Netherlands at Deventer, including the original site on the Ijssel River founded by Gerard Groote, a Dutch Catholic deacon who founded the Brethren (and Sisters) of the Common Life. Groote began this community in the house of his friend and disciple Florentius Radewyns, who was also the town vicar (and leader of a hospice for poor women in his own estate).[26] Deventer became a key medieval intellectual center and, by 1500, the leading center for Dutch printing.

Harry Stout, the Jonathan Edwards Professor of American Religious History at Yale University, also highlights looking through the lens of prominent alumni: "As for 'how to save the Christian college,' the proof is in the product. A selective listing of the Christian College alumni and where they are today would be mind-boggling."[27]

In a sense, associations or alumni of the Sisters and Brethren of the Common Life are also difficult to comprehend. Erasmus alone has works inextricably linked to the study of sixteenth-century

Europe and in various ways influences religious and literary history to this day. In addition to his impact on his era, *The Handbook of a Christian Night*, his Latin and Greek translations of the New Testament, *In Praise of Folly*, and other works are familiar and formative narratives for large swaths of contemporary students.

Although volumes are written about the reach of the Common Life and its connection to influencers, the main point here is they introduced something rather different to the educational flow with waves still reaching shore today. Whether a short stay or long, the waves these alumni initiated looked different after their intersection with Groote's movement. In the case of Erasmus, the intensity of the community life did not hold for him. After three years, Erasmus left to study in Paris, France, Belgium, and England.[28] He later bemoaned monastic austerity and its disdain for the classics. However, what remained with him was the "emphasis on a personal relationship with God."[29] It proves difficult to disconnect his love for Scripture from the Brethren's constant contact with it, even reading it aloud during the students' meals. In his correspondence to his friend John Colet (future dean of St. Paul's Cathedral), he writes, "I cannot tell you, dear Colet, how I hurry on, with all sails set, to holy literature. How I dislike everything that keeps me back, or retards me."[30]

The radical (or uniquely intense) nature of Groote's movement was not the only formative aspect in the lives of its esteemed students like Erasmus as the same proved true for his cofounder Radewyns, who was educated at the University of Prague. Groote had actually met him at Prague and himself had two degrees from the University of Paris. However, the movement's drawing power for participants and lasting impressions on them are notable nonetheless.

We look at Groote's work acknowledging that today's general programs and degrees remain the mainstay of marketing and budgets for many colleges and likely will for the near future. Most residential colleges will deliver credit-bearing courses and experiences in a mélange of media formats instead of traditional seat-time protocol.³¹ Perhaps the key lesson stemming from the Common Life movement, however, is the ability to imagine radical responses to recurring needs. In both the modality and the message, we find Groote's response to needs in the fourteenth-century Netherlands.

Part of what Groote was reimagining was an educational or spiritual development much different from that of the Scholastics (a term popularized by sixteenth-century humanist critics).³² It was not an affront to Thomas Aquinas' *Summa Theologica* from the previous century; indeed, Groote himself had benefited from the university system that stemmed from cathedral schools. Rather, it was Groote's desire to help believers focus more on their service to Christ than their intellectual reflections. Glenn Martin, a regular lecturer for Youth with a Mission, often responded thusly to erudite or cumbersome treatises given to dialectical reasoning: "It's dry as Scholastic dust!"³³—perhaps for good reason based on the sheer quantity of their manuscripts. It is little wonder that many of the bookbinder fragments used for filler in book covers are shredded copies of Scholastics' legal works.³⁴

Groote's efforts were proving radical in various ways. Though his hospices appeared monastic in their rigors of common living, they allowed membership without taking irrevocable vows. In other words, most remained laypersons. Groote imagined a different way to a similar end in the tumultuous fourteenth century as the landscape of civilizations was being refashioned, let alone the landscape of education.

It is apparent the movement itself, not unlike satellite churches today stemming from a megachurch, was fueled by Groote's unique gifts and background. He was a lay preacher who attracted followers—and large crowds—through his sermons on spiritual regeneration. He aligned with a movement of popular piety, more commonly called "mysticism." That reality was not without precedent. The German Dominican mystic Meister Eckhart (d. 1337) gained a considerable number of followers through the work of nuns who transposed his sermons into devotional books (and a century before Gutenberg). During his time with the Carthusians, he contemplated giving his life to solitude, but they rejected this because of his strong speaking skills and need to use them.

The mystics called for Christ, not priests, in structured confessions, as the central mediator between God and their souls. In 1374, Groote founded a religious sisterhood, which was followed by more numerous establishments for men. His intent was not to replace the education of his day but to enhance it around a specific mission—offering it in a different format. It was indeed a radical departure for his day (sort of like many of the reimagined modalities today).

The men would call themselves the Brothers (Brethren) of the Common Life and would eventually receive papal approval for their mode of living. As their influence spread throughout Germany, they opened schools that taught a Christian ideal of character and behavior, accenting their lessons in reading and writing. Their pedagogy paid less attention to systematic doctrine and more to personal qualities such as humility, neighborly love, tolerance, reverence, and conscientiousness in the performance of duty.[35]

Radical ideas, loud voices, or enlarged platforms often draw the ire of the status quo. It was no different for Groote as the clergy revoked Groote's preaching license in 1383, the year before his death. Radical ideas, however, are not inherently brash or friction leaning. Inextricably linked to Groote's imagination of a different way of kingdom service was the establishment of *Devotio Moderna* or the Modern Devotion.[36] This movement not only spread throughout parts of Europe (and perhaps provided the context for the Protestant Reformation and Catholic Reformation) but also resurfaced among millennials in the present era. However, it is best understood in its context—"the long fifteenth century" (1370s–1530s).[37]

Groote did not take a traditional path from his college degrees to implementing a business or an organization, nor did he stay long in any guild. Rather, he went through a near-death experience that opened his eyes to the ephemeral nature of his inherited wealth (he was orphaned at age ten). He bequeathed much of his family wealth to the care of the Carthusians of Monnikhuizen, with whom he lived for three years. He also presented the deed of his family mansion to the city of Deventer. "The Deed contained instructions to turn his home into a hospice for poor women who sought shelter and wished to serve God. The clause in the deed— 'who wish to serve God'—became the signature phrase for the movement [which at the time was not in the picture]."[38]

Among the most influential voices of his Carthusian colleagues was Jan van Ruysbroeck, a Brabant mystic and author of *The Spiritual Espousals*. Groote's prolonged visit with him in Groenendael in present-day Belgium proved formative.[39] Ruysbroeck's simplicity was a pleasant surprise, and his three stages of the spiritual life were promising in leading fellow Christians away from the staid formalism of the Church to personal devotion—from the moral to the interior (spiritual) man. Ruysbroeck taught and wrote in the vernacular, a radical break from religious teachers and a practice that would help revolutionize the Common Life movement. He also applied it to his use of Benedict's *lectio divina*, especially in personal journaling.[40]

In reimagining today's educational landscape with this historic example in mind, we see some key components:

(1) a gifted speaker
(2) an intense spiritual compass
(3) a clear mission
(4) a vision for what could improve the training experiences for pastors
(5) a reimagined approach to spiritual development
(6) a "published" version of one's views (still in manuscript form for Ruysbroeck and Groote)
(7) financial backing (at first it was Groote's own, bequeathed)
(8) a new modality—the use of the vernacular languages
(9) a new "certification" for laity

His schools also introduced the eight-grade system that revolutionized the educational enterprise. The same proved true with introducing the *trivium* and *quadrivium* at pre-university levels, which prepared their students for the next step while concomitantly introducing the humanities into these lower levels. His schools also had a built-in work program to help sustain their operations—copying manuscripts and, after the Gutenberg press, book printing.[41]

Groote did not live to see a lot of the Common Life's success. The Brethren of Common Life school in Zwolle boasted 1,200 students within a generation of his passing (under rector John Cele, 1375–1417). A century after his passing, however, the Deventer school had two thousand students.

Just as Benedict of Nursia and Gerard Groote looked for new ways to invest their callings and commitments in the education needs of their times, more recently Christians have tried to reimagine the educational status quo. We stand on the shoulders of some formidable leaders as we think of the formation of some modern collective responses to recurring needs within Christian education—and its value to the betterment of society.

As of 2022, those graduating with at least a bachelor's degree have growing advantages financially over those without degrees. The Pew Research Center reports the gap is widening in numerous ways.[42] However, a key question remains: what is the purpose of Christian education in this journey to vocational success? For life? Many individuals and organizations have addressed this, and new ones continue to do so in new ways.

On the one hand, we have the robust Council of Christian Colleges and Universities (CCCU), formed in 1976, and very recently upstart associations such as the International Association of College Educators (IACE). On the other hand, we have new college models and associations attached to some of the world's largest churches, such as Highlands College based in Birmingham, Alabama. With 420 graduates in 2021 alone, it surpasses many of the CCCU member institutions in the total number of graduates.[43]

Such a comparison is not apples to apples, but its graduates are from the same orchard—Christian churches. We also have Thirdmill (Third Millennium Ministries, Inc.), whose bold motto is "Biblical Education. For the World. For Free." Since its 1997 founding, it has amassed more than two hundred partners globally, expanded resources into more than twenty languages, and taught more than a million students, and it has an option for credit via Thirdmill Seminary (completely online for $125 a credit): "Our mission is to prepare Christian leaders to lead a transformation of the world into God's Kingdom by providing biblical education, for the world, for free."[44] Imagination in the education space has many new faces and places.

The CCCU now boasts of more than 185 college members, ninety thousand faculty and staff members, and a half million students, yet it is also an organization like the others mentioned that is dealing with the stark realities of national educational downturns.[45] For decades, the enrollment gurus of Christian colleges tracked the bubble of students coming through grades K–12 and knew the very years the bonanza would dissipate. One of the formative marketing minds for the Apollo Group and two-time vice president at Indiana Wesleyan University (formerly Marion College), Jerry Shepherd, argued in 1988, "I think this non-traditional format is the future. It's exciting to be a part of something that could change and sustain Christian higher education."[46] He certainly was correct, and we need other Shepherds for what is next.

In addition, Pew Research Center data showing the numbers of their parents either leaving the Church altogether or having stopped attending is alarming. The effect on their children's college choices is now part of the enrollment mix. Pew began sharing the numbers of these alarming drops more than a decade ago, and we find ourselves not only in a chaotic economic situation and cultural war but also with a markedly smaller pool of applicants.[47]

The enrollment issue is not particular to Christian universities, as it is capturing headlines of a wide array of media outlets.[48]

The National Student Clearinghouse Research Center records that "public institutions suffered the brunt" of recent enrollment losses, down 9.4 percent since the onset of the COVID-19 pandemic.[49]

Imagination rooted in our clear Christ-centered moorings is needed. The educational landscape is not too different from the waves rippling at its base—the churches and their affiliations. In the past, and likely for the near future, some leaders of churches (still the main source of students flowing to the CCCU schools) jumped to forming new denominations. The Center for the Study of Global Christianity claims some forty-five thousand different Christian denominations globally and some two hundred in the United States.[50] From early Christianity through colonial America, a litany of issues has prompted religious groups to drive the proverbial stake in the ground and rally like-minded others around it, a topic outlined even by the popular *Live Science* site.[51] Add the cluster of megachurches and their followings, such as Church of the Highlands, and you find a mélange of new faces in the educational arena.

The Church of the Highlands runs forty thousand per Sunday in its services. Its web tagline is: "Church of the Highlands is a life-giving church meeting in multiple locations throughout Alabama and West Georgia." It launched Highlands University in 2011, which already has some one thousand alumni (mostly church ministers) involved in 250 ministries in thirty-four states and ten countries.[52] Such details offer only part of the picture. Its founder, Pastor Chris Hodges, first launched ARC (the Association of Related Churches), and Highlands was its first plant. Now ARC is one of its main partnerships with 1,036 founded churches in numerous countries.[53] He also founded GROW, another partnership, which has proven to help a host of churches "to reach more people faster."[54]

Highlands is only one of the concerted efforts among Christian academic ranks to deal with millennial preferences. As exciting as this movement is, the brightest star in the academic arena remains the Council for Christian Colleges and Universities, with its history chronicled in *The Shining Lights.*[55] However, before we look at this, perhaps it is in order to note that another stake is being pounded into receptive soil among the smaller and a few of the most conservative of the CCCU members (and now several former CCCU members)—the founding of the IACE.

Prima facie, like the various denominations, IACE seems to be duplicating at a much smaller level some (a couple of the many dozens) of the offerings already in place with the CCCU. In addition, its trajectory is somewhat aligned with more conservative missions like the International Christian Education Association (ICEA), founded in 1946 to serve "churches and para-church organizations by providing conventions, conferences, institutes, workshops and seminars designed to equip Christians for life, leadership, and ministry."[56] Already, with just a glimpse of the imagination of the Church in the education space, we see the dizzying manifestation of creative responses in the assortment of similar acronyms! If we venture further into the international educational landscape, we take on others such as INCHE (International Network for Christian Higher Education, which until 2018 was IAPCHE).[57]

Is the same stake being driven into soil trod by the same shrinking audiences? First, IACE's name is similar to yet another much older group, Christian Educators Association International (CEAI), founded in 1953 in Pasadena, California. All of these organizations have overlapping parts of their missions and similar orthodox creedal statements.[58] However, CEAI focuses on Christians in the public schools—though certainly its mission statement and offerings could benefit like-minded professors anywhere—and ICEA targets church leaders and settings. Acknowledging these realities, we will look at two missions alongside each other (IACE's and CCCU's):

IACE's mission is to unify, synergize, and strengthen collective conviction around biblical orthodoxy and orthopraxy, cultural witness, scholarship, professional excellence, and resourcing of Christian education at all levels.[59]

> [The CCCU's mission] We are committed to support-
> ing, protecting, and promoting the value of integrating
> the Bible—divinely inspired, true, and authoritative—
> throughout all curricular and cocurricular aspects of the
> educational experience on our campuses, including teach-
> ing and research. We support a coherent approach to edu-
> cation in which the development of the mind, spirit, body,
> and emotions are seamlessly woven together in the quest
> not just for knowledge but also for wisdom.[60]

Their visions linked to operational realities seem similar, though
the robustness of the CCCU has a litany of actual programs in
place, while IACE is nascent but operational.

> [IACE] Functioning as a network and umbrella organi-
> zation, the IACE will seek to provide enablement, con-
> nections, and collaborative opportunities for the various
> aspects of Christian education.

> [The CCCU's section on "Academic Excellence" and
> "Three Pillars"] Through an array of initiatives, we pro-
> mote the development of high-quality academic research
> projects, provide opportunities for faculty to conduct
> innovative research with peers from other campuses, and
> provide administrators with opportunities . . . To fulfill our
> mission and meet the needs of our institutions, we provide
> unique services for administration, faculty, students, and
> friends of Christian higher education in three pillars of
> strategic focus ["Public Advocacy," "Professional Develop-
> ment & Scholarship," and "Experiential Education"].

Atop this, let us pause and compare Highlands College's mission
and vision:

> [Mission] Highlands College is a biblical higher education
> institution that exists to supply the Church with leaders of

competence, character, and spiritual maturity, holistically trained to lead lives of eternal impact by fulfilling the Great Commission.

[**Vision**] Our vision is to create a ministry academy model, applying leading-edge methods in world-class facilities, where students graduate debt-free—educated, equipped, and empowered to expand the Kingdom of God in a complex and changing world.[61]

As we exercise imagination for Christ's mission and how to orchestrate and enhance educational efforts to do so, hope is also found in what is happening among self-professed Christian universities at the undergraduate level. Perry Glanzer, professor at Baylor University and editor-in-chief of *Christian Scholar's Review*, addresses this issue. In discussing the largest twenty-three Christian colleges enrolling two-fifths of the CCCU students, he notes:

> On the undergraduate level, however, there is cause for hope. All but two (91%) require two Christian courses and 14 of the 23 require three or more. Furthermore, 18 of the 23 institutions (78%) use Christian theological reasoning in their conduct code. In contrast, high church Protestant denominations dominate our list of largely secularized institutions that do not even require a Christian course or use Christian theological reasoning in their conduct codes. In undergraduate education, we probably should be most concerned about the future numbers and Christian vitality of high church Protestant institutions.[62]

Like many other strong voices on the issue of higher education, Glanzer is looking not at whether they are self-identified Christian universities but at whether they "provide a strong theological contribution (what I call Christ animating learning)."[63] We circle back to Bonhoeffer's notion of mission, of an aspiration to be with

God in more meaningful ways, and aspiration to help others to find the centrality of God in their routines and institutions.

Russell Moore addresses this in *Onward: Engaging the Culture without Losing the Gospel*: "Our call is to an *engaged alienation*, a Christianity that preserves the distinctiveness of our gospel while not retreating from our callings as neighbors, and friends, and citizens."[64] The moniker for this book could be his statement, "But while we are a Kingdom First people, we are not a Kingdom Only people" (based in part on Matt 6:33).[65]

James Davison Hunter reminds us that Jesus gave his followers the great commission to "go into all the world" (Mark 16:15) and that the commission can be interpreted more than geographically—to faraway places. It can also "be interpreted in terms of social structure. The church is to go into all realms of social life."[66] This message comes with both marching orders, so to speak, and caution, as popular preachers and authors like Tony Evans address often.[67] He challenges his listeners to do good "in the midst of darkness, fear and hate."[68] For Christian education at all levels, we need to imbibe this Janus-faced mission of looking across the pews and across the street: "The future of Christian social witness cannot assume the gospel, but must articulate it explicitly and coherently."[69]

While all but one of the largest twenty-three Christian institutions are in the low-church Protestant traditions, retaining for the most part Christ-animated teaching/learning, his research team also found an alarming trend at the graduate level:

> These low-church Protestant institutions may be growing, but it is not clear they really offer graduate education that is all that different from pluralistic universities. Low-church graduate education will need to figure out how Christ can animate graduate education, if Christian higher education is going to prosper.[70]

One key exception to this reality is seminaries, especially seminaries partnering with and/or planting overseas institutions. Though the American market remains volatile, positive gains are surfacing among new and refashioned seminaries. For example, Wesley Seminary in Indiana[71] was founded in 2009 and has enjoyed steady gains to more than five hundred students from twenty-seven countries in 2022 and partners with a variety of overseas institutions, especially in the explosive area of church growth in sub-Saharan Africa.[72] This is but one of the growing seminaries, and it joins many other vibrant seminaries committed to the theological substance for which Glanzer is searching.[73]

As imagination calls for biblically centered and spiritually centric approaches for a new generation of colleges in the current context, we realize through the kaleidoscopic lenses like that of the emergent movement (mainly in the 1990s and early 2000s) that Christian higher education will take on more diverse forms with each passing decade. Biola University's Ed Stetzer[74] categorizes the emerging movement's theology and practice: "Relevants" attempt to contextualize worship and message while remaining theologically conservative and biblically based. "Reconstructionists" are largely concerned with church structures and may lean toward a house church model for church life. "Revisionists" reject the historic form of the Church and the gospel and revise biblical stances on issues such as gender roles, homosexuality, and the authority of Scripture.[75] A large swath of readers (the majority of evangelicals) consider themselves outside the waning emergent movement. Many are far afield from Emergent Village and its early leaders such as Brian McLaren.[76] However, the implications of imagination will continue to manifest themselves in diverse ways among the body of Christ.

For the Christian educator, wherever we are on this spectrum we can take notes from Glanzer on how we can imagine new approaches or enhance those already in place: "To see oneself and one's students in light of an overarching cosmic drama with God as the central character of the story transforms these teachers' vision of themselves, and their students."[77]

As we imagine and lean into what Glanzer sees as Christ-animated learning (a theme throughout the *Christian Scholar's*

Review blog posts he edits), considering options ranging from the traditional evangelical (likely low-church) CCCU colleges to Thirdmill Seminary and Highlands College may prove beneficial. At education's extreme, the seminary or Bible degree on an iPhone via influencers like Pastor Tony Evans (e.g., Tony Evans Training Center) may even merit consideration.[78] At $19.99 a month, Evans' imaginative offering is a factor in saving a Christian college even if a creatively successful approach to furthering the general mission of Christian education resides just beyond the horizon.

Imagination Explored

An imagination rooted in the aspiration of Christian discipleship is defined by a number of common qualities (being relational, purposeful, and hopeful). A number of institutional variables then also need to influence a planning process. Below please find questions we encourage a Christian college to consider during this particular phase of such a process.

- *First, how does a Christian college cultivate the imagination of various members of its community? Among curricular educators? Cocurricular educators? Students?*

A Christian college, however implicit such an effort may be, navigates the present and future challenges based upon an exercise of imagination. Such an imagination is not stagnant but always in some sort of flux. For this reason, the response to a challenge facing a Christian college today may be slightly different, however incremental that difference may be, when facing the same challenge the next day.

Assuming a sense of awareness of the existence of such an imagination, how intentional is a Christian college in the cultivation of the imagination among members of its community? Due to the subtle nature of its cultivation, such a process is rarely linear and singular in direction. Quite often, mixed messages and conflicting practices influence such an imagination. Leaders may not be able to eliminate those challenges in their totality. However, an awareness of how a Christian college's imagination is being cultivated can greatly reduce the possibility.

In addition, how does a Christian college cultivate the imagination of various components of its community? Curricular educators, cocurricular educators, and students, for example, populate different sectors of a Christian college and play different roles. In such matters, uniformity is never the goal. However, the health of a Christian college is measured in larger part by a spirit of unity. As a result, any effort to deduce how a Christian college cultivates the imagination needs to focus not only on all members of the community but also on the different roles those members play within that community.

- *Second, how is that imagination aligned with a particular aspiration of discipleship?*

Once a Christian college identifies how it cultivates the imagination of members of its community, its critical next step involves grappling with the level with which that imagination is aligned with a particular vision of discipleship. Such an effort assumes an underlying awareness of a particular aspiration of discipleship. As mentioned in the previous chapter, such an aspiration needs to reflect an understanding of discipleship befitting a Christian college. Realizing that Christian colleges take on a variety of forms, such an understanding needs to be nuanced based upon, for example, an institution's Christian tradition and organizational type.

The planning process then needs to grapple with how well the imagination being exercised is an extension of that understanding of discipleship. As noted under the previous question, the possibility of that extension being perfect in nature is unlikely due to the sheer number and fluid nature of variables. But the chance of success a Christian college has with the planning process is greatly increased by an awareness of that alignment.

For example, imagining the establishment of a Reserve Officers' Training Corps as part of a planning process may mesh with the aspiration of discipleship animating one campus while feeling askew to the aspiration animating a second. Being aware of that aspiration and the quality of its alignment with imagination being leveraged in a particular planning process is the important factor. Among planning processes involving organizational units, *uniformity* is never the key. In contrast, *unity* proves critical.

- *Third, how are members of the community prepared to integrate worship with their work?*

One way to assess the alignment of the aspiration of discipleship with the imagination is to explore how well members of the community are prepared to integrate worship with their work. Regardless of their roles on campus, all members of the campus community should be able to view their work as an extension of worship and perhaps even as an act of worship. Common worship services, Bible studies, and praise and worship offerings, to name only three, are opportunities to fulfill what it means to be created in God's image and offer praise to the Creator. But such practices all serve a further purpose in preparing the imagination of the community. Too often such practices are viewed as separate from curricular practices and even other cocurricular practices. Such perceptions then have a considerable impact upon the imagination and its ability to inform planning processes.

- *Fourth, being created in God's image, in what way is the imagination as exercised relational? Purposeful? Hopeful?*

As planning processes unfold, one of the most critical set of questions that needs to be asked is: What is the quality of the relational nature such an imagination would inspire? What is the quality of its purposeful nature? The quality of its hopeful nature?

All too often, the relational nature of the imagination is pro forma. In essence, individuals populating planning efforts may be stacked with like-minded people. When feedback is requested from larger segments of the community, the feedback that emerges, while acknowledged, is ultimately ignored. In whatever ways prove most profitable for a particular planning process, the strength of its relational nature impacts the strength of the imagination being brought to bear.

Comparable questions also need to be asked about the purposeful nature of the planning process. Planning processes, while potentially life-giving exercises for a Christian college, can also become exercises completed out of obligation. Participants should clearly believe they are participating in a process for a particular reason. How can a Christian college cultivate such a belief? By ensuring that the process and corresponding imagination are an extension of an animating atmosphere of discipleship.

Finally, even when a Christian college is under threat in any number of possible ways, it is important to assess the hopeful nature of the imagination being exercised in a planning process. Fear can often parade as purpose, but fear ultimately gives itself away as a reaction to a perceived threat. On the other hand, purpose identifies a proactive path by which a particular program unit or even the institution can thrive amid the pressures of a world in which it does not belong. Although a time can and should be set aside to identify and contend with those threats, those times in the end allow for an institution to remain focused on exercising the hopeful nature of its imagination.

- *Fifth, what particular programs, if any, are designed to form a relational imagination? A purposeful imagination? A hopeful imagination?*

In many ways, a planning process is the result of an imagination fostered long before a process ever begins. While created in God's image, participants this side of eternity are not always inherently relational, purposeful, and hopeful. The temper of the present age cuts against all three of those qualities of what it means to be created in God's image and to exercise a rightly formed imagination. As a result, a Christian college needs to ask itself, before, during, and even after a planning process, what particular programs, if any, are designed to form a relational imagination? A purposeful imagination? A hopeful imagination? In the same sense, a Christian college needs to ask: What internal and external pressures are challenging such programming and, in turn, the desired outcomes of a relational, purposeful, and hopeful imagination?

* * *

The imagination informing a planning process is, we trust, the result of a clearly articulated and well-practiced understanding of an aspiration for discipleship. Aided by the presence of the Holy Spirit, such an imagination, regardless of the particular planning process, will prove relational, purposeful, and hopeful even in the face of considerable challenges. The outcomes may prove far greater than could be imagined before the process began.

Excellence in unique yet widely recognizable forms is the outgrowth of such an imagination. As with Gideon, a Christian college must ask whether members of its community are willing to meet the challenge before them. Such a challenge may prove difficult. Such a demand may provide previously unanticipated growth in specific areas. Such a challenge may mean risking failure. The answers to those questions, however, are the results of an imagination straining to sense where God may be calling next.

3

Collaboration

In Dietrich Bonhoeffer's Trinity Church sermon text (Judg 6:15–16; 7:2; 8:23), God told Gideon to send home sizable portions of the army that Gideon had assembled. Even so, Dietrich Bonhoeffer wanted the congregants who joined him on that Sunday in Berlin to know they were not alone.

Gideon obeyed God and gave "up the only forces that, from a human perspective, he could count on, here in the face of an enemy."[1] Obviously, Bonhoeffer's congregants would want to know why God would make such a demand—why God is "always standing in human beings' ways and frustrating their own plans."[2] Bonhoeffer proposes that this "wild God" might be "zealous for his own honor."[3] In the end, however, Bonhoeffer looks to God as one who wants to share in a properly ordered relationship with creation and, in particular, with the creature God called to have dominion over all other creatures.

If pride in one's own achievements is even possible, such a relationship cannot exist. Bonhoeffer contends that "human beings keep getting it wrong" and that "God is opposed to the proud."[4] Repeatedly, the temptation calls—to try "for our own credit," regardless of how small the aspiration may be. To succumb to that temptation would result in a disordered relationship. If Gideon's army, however insignificant it proved to be in comparison to the Midianites', was victorious, the temptation would be to gloat in their own might. However seemingly preposterous, God's declarations to Gideon that day precluded even the possibility that the coming victory would be one secured by might.

With the Third Reich gaining in strength right outside the church doors on that day in February 1933, Bonhoeffer wanted to assure his congregants that might was not what proved critical. They were, in fact, called to surrender—not to the Nazis but to the God who wanted more than anything to be in right relationship with them, right beside them regardless of the horror that might emerge in the coming weeks, months, and years.

Perhaps the most critical line in Bonhoeffer's sermon then reads, "[Gideon] believed, he obeyed, he gave God the glory, he renounced the honor for himself, and God kept the promise made."[5] A properly ordered imagination reveals that God's grace, not human might, is the greatest weapon one could wield.

Residing in the backdrop of Bonhoeffer's reading of Gideon's story is that Christ forged that weapon on Good Friday. The Old Testament records how God repeatedly reached out to the creature whom God gave dominion over all other creatures. Gideon, as with other heroes of the faith, heeded God's calling. Others, even if it might have proved sufficient this side of eternity, chose not to heed God's calling.

Bonhoeffer wants his congregants by faith to embrace God's grace as sufficient in the face of any challenge. They do not collaborate with God as equals; nonetheless, God is by their side, waging wars only grace can win. Bonhoeffer thus contends, "Let God alone, let the word and the sacraments and the commandment of God be your weapons; don't look around for other help; don't be frightened. God is with you. 'Let my grace be sufficient for you.'"[6] Whatever success humans find this side of eternity, grace abounds in the hope that success beyond imagination finds its fullness in eternity.

What is less obvious yet made possible by grace is Bonhoeffer's emerging ecclesiology or emerging understanding of the Church.

For reasons noted in previous chapters, Bonhoeffer believes Gideon's story is also the Church's story. Bonhoeffer reminds his congregants of this point in his sermon by asking, "Is this a tall tale like all the others?" His response then reads, "Anyone who says so has failed to understand that Gideon is still with us, that the old story of Gideon is being played out in Christendom every day."[7] The Church, in contrast to a culture that selectively wraps Christ around socially acceptable norms, is for whom the theological commitments defining Gideon's story hold true.

As a result, Bonhoeffer's congregants were to cast their gaze in both horizontal and vertical directions. Grace was made possible by Christ's sacrifice and made available by the Holy Spirit. Part of what Bonhoeffer argues is that grace also exists in all who gather as Christ's body, who order their lives according to the theological truths found in the stories of faithful exemplars such as Gideon. The Church then becomes the community in which the eternal gives meaning to the temporal. For the Church, "the word and the sacraments and the commandment of God" become their weapons. The question then is not the size of the army but the practices that shape its theological imagination.

When reflecting on the ethics of Dietrich Bonhoeffer, theologian Stanley Hauerwas argues, "In performance Christians are called to recognize time aright, to attune themselves to a time that is God's time. The context in which this attunement occurs is properly called worship."[8] Worship made it possible for Bonhoeffer's congregants to see one another as people sitting next to each other in a common physical space. In contrast, Bonhoeffer's congregants, like all who gather in Christ's name, take on the calling to be Christ's body, to live out Christ's sacrifice, in whatever circumstances they find themselves. Drawing again from Bonhoeffer, Hauerwas contends that, in worship, "time is not so much forgotten, erased, or transcended as it is radically altered."[9] That radical alteration allows what was previously regarded "as the standard measurement of time to be converted and reconfigured by what God's time shows itself truly to be."[10]

When Bonhoeffer poses the question of with whom Christians collaborate, the answer is not only first and foremost God but also all people for whom the word, sacraments, and commandments of God order their lives. Perhaps Bonhoeffer's most elaborate understanding of the Church, however, is found in one of the works he was preparing but tragically never completed. In what became his *Letters and Papers from Prison*, we find an "Outline for a Book" on ecclesiology that he sketched shortly before being executed by the Nazis. Despite the circumstances around him, perhaps not that different from the circumstances Gideon faced, "the prisoner is focused on the very nature of the people who follow Christ." Perhaps the most enigmatic phrase Bonhoeffer left in those papers is: "The church is only the church when it is there for others."[11] Such an understanding rightfully includes the Church being of service to others, in particular, the most vulnerable as articulated throughout Scripture. Such an understanding also rightfully includes the Church forging collaborative relationships with other individuals and institutions in a common effort to bear witness to the grace only God could offer:

> Then the LORD God said, "It is not good that the man should be alone; I will make him a helper fit for him." . . . So the LORD God caused a deep sleep to fall upon the man, and while he slept took one of his ribs and closed up its place with flesh; and the rib which the LORD God had taken from the man he made into a woman and brought her to the man. Then the man said, "This at last is bone of my bones and flesh of my flesh; she shall be called Woman, because she was taken out of Man."[12]
> Genesis 2:18, 21–23 (RSV)

While college leaders often extol the virtues of collaboration, the institutions they lead remain notoriously resistant to such encouragement. Even colleagues who are sympathetic are often "locked into institutional structures and cultures"[13] that mitigate against collaboration. Despite the preponderance of research touting its impact on student learning, team teaching courses often prove just as difficult to staff as they prove financially to reward. When it comes time for promotion and tenure, being the single author of an article or book is worth more than being a coauthor—especially a second author. Reflective of the reductionistic impulse that led to their emergence, academic departments on even the smallest campuses often become warring factions—especially when budgets grow tight. At almost every turn, the "structures, processes, and routines" defining academic life from the individual to organizational level "prevent collaboration."[14]

No stranger to the impulse animating the research university, Bonhoeffer viewed human beings called to the pursuit of truth as being participants in an inherently collaborative endeavor. Woven into Bonhoeffer's understanding of the life of Gideon as detailed in Judges 6:15–16; 7:2; 8:23 is a theological anthropology Bonhoeffer offered in the lectures that became *Creation and Fall*. No sooner had God created Adam than God acted on the understanding that "it is not good that man should be alone." Reflecting upon such an understanding, Bonhoeffer writes, "Adam is alone in anticipation of the other person, of community."[15] Adam was incomplete when alone. Adam, as with all who would follow, was created to be in community with God and others of his kind. In Adam, Bonhoeffer finds one who "was alone in hope"[16]—a hope God would soon fulfill with the creation of Eve and the propagation of humanity.

As detailed in previous chapters, Bonhoeffer's reading of Genesis 1–4:1 is theological and, in turn, inherently christological. As a result, this image of Adam as being alone summons in Bonhoeffer the recognition that Christ was physically and metaphysically alone at the time of his crucifixion, because "Christ alone loves the other person, because Christ is the way by which the human race has returned to its creator." In contrast, human beings are alone, because "we have pushed other people away from us, because we have hated them."[17] In our created fullness, human beings are inherently collaborative and serve one another in the role of "suitable helper." In our depravity, we push "other people away from us," believing, albeit in futility, we are sufficient when we are alone.

Bonhoeffer would thus contend that a properly ordered understanding of discipleship is inherently collaborative for both individuals and the institutions they populate. Despite how we may order our days, God created us to see the presence of other people in our lives as gifts. For this very reason, a proper understanding of diversity is rooted in the reality that each person is created in God's image and thus, each in one's own way, reflects qualities of the Creator. The reflection of the qualities of the Creator grows incrementally as we strive to appreciate one another. Regardless of how we may strive to isolate ourselves, our well-being as individuals is inextricably tied to the well-being of others in our community reflected this side of eternity in the body of Christ.

Bonhoeffer contends that Adam "does not know how it happens. But Adam knows that God has made use of the human, has taken a piece of the sleeping human body and has formed the other person from it. And it is with a true cry of joy that Adam recognizes the woman."[18] Eve's presence is not a burden to Adam but a gift, just as Adam's presence to Eve will also become a gift. When sin weaves its way into their lives, Adam and Eve come to view each other as persons upon whom to project blame, not persons with whom to share in accepting responsibility. Regardless of what is to come, Bonhoeffer lobbies, "That Eve is derived from Adam is a cause not for pride, but for particular gratitude, with Adam."[19]

Theologians understandably look to this passage as being critical in the development of an understanding of marriage. For our purposes, we theologically view Adam and Eve as archetypes for the relations all beings created in God's image were called to share. With this end in mind, Bonhoeffer stresses that Adam and Eve

from their origin have been one, and only in becoming one do they return to their origin. But this becoming one never means the merging of two or the abolition of their creatureliness as individuals. It actualizes the highest possible degree of belonging to each other, which is based precisely on their being different from one another.[20]

As a result, the qualities that make each human being unique are just as critical to efforts to collaborate as what individuals hold in common.

For Bonhoeffer, this understanding of what it means to be human yields at least two considerations important to us as we move toward an understanding of the critical nature of collaboration among humans—especially humans who populate the Christian college. First, Bonhoeffer argues that collaboration is the context in which we learn that we possess limits and, in turn, can be truly free. This stands in contrast to a more common understanding of what it means to be human and, in turn, free—that humans can overcome any number of challenges by sheer force of will; the best possible understanding of freedom is then perceived as being the absence of as many constraints as possible. In this scenario, a limitless understanding of human potential fuels, for example, an understanding of academic freedom as solely defined by an unfettered ability to follow truth wherever it may lead.

Bonhoeffer contends that when humans live in isolation from one another, the illusion of infinite potential becomes all too alluring. When humans live in even the thinnest of communities, we quickly realize that someone is always more talented than we are—whatever that talent may be—if for no other reason than our talents exist at their peak for but a few fleeting moments. Refusing to embrace the illusion of the human agent's unlimited potential, Bonhoeffer argues, "Adam lived as one who received the divine gift [of Eve] with pure faith and sight. The Creator knows that this free life as a creature can be borne within its limit only if it is loved."[21] In such a context, human beings recognize not only their limitations but also that others called into their lives can aid in the pursuit to be free. The talents we possess are not to be hoarded as aids to our own achievement but offered as means to the betterment of others and, in turn, ourselves.

Unfortunately, the threat posed by COVID-19 offers a tragic example of what happens when human beings, even those who are experts in related areas, refuse to acknowledge their limits, listen to one another, and challenge a virus that has posed a threat to humanity without passion or prejudice. COVID-19 was a biological phenomenon. COVID-19, however, was also an economic, political, and theological phenomenon. As the pandemic progressed, one of the greatest community challenges was the inability of virologists, economists, policymakers, and pastors to acknowledge their respective limitations, search for others who could help mitigate those limitations, and collaborate on solutions.

The Christian college should be a place that forms people habitually to acknowledge what they know as well as what they do not know. Truth in its full form will never be known this side of eternity. According to Bonhoeffer, what truth can be known in its highest form is the result of a "common bearing of the limit by the first two persons [Adam and Eve] in community."[22] To see more clearly, human beings need first to know they presently "see in a mirror dimly."[23] Collaboration brings such a recognition to the surface alongside the recognition that together we can come closer to bearing the created image of God than we can alone.

Second, Bonhoeffer argues that collaboration is the context in which character is forged. Drawing further upon the relationship shared by Adam and Eve, Bonhoeffer notes that "at the point where love for the other is obliterated, a human being can only hate [their limits as finite beings]. A person then desires only, in an unbounded way, to possess the other or destroy the other."[24] In denial of the limitations defining the human condition, Bonhoeffer contends, we view the other as a threat, not an aid. Our own immortality, contingent upon our perception of the efforts we make, must be ours and ours alone.

As a side note, one must wonder what Bonhoeffer, as the Third Reich was ascending to power, sensed regarding the near future of his native Germany. Speculation becomes even more tempting when he writes, "What the human being until now accepted humbly [in terms of one's limitations] at this point becomes a cause for pride and rebellion."[25]

In contrast, Bonhoeffer extols the virtues forged in moments when humans acknowledge their limits and turn to others in a spirit of collaboration. When making such a point, Bonhoeffer lobbies, "The grace of the other person's being our helper . . . a partner because he or she helps bear our limit, that is[,] helps us to live before God."[26] With that understanding in mind, Bonhoeffer even goes so far as to contend, "We can only live before God in community with our helper."[27]

Such an understanding of what it means to be human and, in turn, live in community is the soil out of which the intellectual, moral, and theological virtues grow. While all of the virtues are inextricably tied to one another, we will pause at this point only to inquire as to how the Christian college might be different if the intellectual virtue of humility were to flourish.[28] What more might we be able to learn about the world around us and the God who created it if we collaborated with one another? What more might we be able to learn about ourselves? Perhaps acknowledging the imperfections that mark each one of us is the very ground out of which greater perceptions of truth grow.

Collaboration Exemplified

In our common church history prior to the Protestant split, *cathedral* was the moniker for "the high seat" of spiritual and ecclesiastical authority for a specified geographic region. In England, a cathedral was (and is) one of two key ways to obtain the status of a "city."[29] Cathedrals were important and for many reasons.

Today boundaries seem fluid for most aspects of the Church, especially in higher education. Catholic universities recruit internationally and well beyond their religious ranks. Few Protestant denominational networks still have geographical territories for student recruitment; even so, they hope students worldwide will find their online offerings attractive. As futurist Bryan Alexander reminds us, open education is "triumphant" with open resources, publications, and software becoming the norm.[30]

Although today's landscape varies widely in some ways from the heyday of medieval cathedrals, we find in the development of cathedral schools lessons to accent our strategies for saving the Christian college—especially with "Open Education Triumphant."[31] A key aspect of this example and suggestion, again viewed through Bonhoeffer's theology, is collaboration.

He turns the common idea of today's collaboration on its head. Rather than noting people merely reaching across an aisle to join hands, Bonhoeffer first sees people on the same side of the aisle joining hearts before God. Instead of seeing what collaborators have in common, he looks at how to deal with their limitations since the fall.

Bonhoeffer chronicles Eden—a search for knowledge—as a misuse of collaboration, prodded by a warped serpentine imagination. When Bonhoeffer highlights Adam and Eve being wholly committed to each other, part of the beauty of this manifestation of providence is "precisely based upon their being different from one another." They worked the rest of their lives to confront in tandem the limitations of their depravity, not trying to transcend it.

In education, we often look for simple checklists—but for Bonhoeffer the only thing that was simple is the fulcrum of his faith and his theology. Bonhoeffer's preoccupation is similar here to Hugh of St. Victor in Paris in the twelfth century, as focusing on becoming (or "reforming") ourselves into "dwelling places" of God.[32] Bonhoeffer sees us ultimately as vessels, and by extension our Christian institutions and collaborations should manifest such a mindset. He finds God's design at the beginning and end of our planning and with that design, our differences and the astounding possibilities of a rightly ordered imagination.

Is there a more appropriate arena in which to invoke a theology of our decisions than in institutions of higher learning? After all, modern universities began with one subject as the queen of the sciences—theology. Western colleges after Rome's fall (and many Eastern) began as enterprises of one faith—Christianity.[33]

God has created us to use our imaginations to complement one another. As we look at the cathedral schools, we find some takeaways of this collaborative endeavor between the Church and city, between the sacred and the secular (as the Church had defined it).[34]

Similar to the founding of Harvard, Princeton, and the story of the founding of the United States, the earliest manifestations of religious schools in the fifth and sixth centuries were utilitarian; they simultaneously met the needs of the Church and of greater society. In the early Middle Ages, they also stepped into a space that the secular institutions no longer could. The Roman infrastructure was but a shadow of its heyday. To have literate priests and accountants and clerks for the wide-reaching church involvement, they began their own feeder system.

We do not have the space here to chronicle this development from its beginning to the time of Charlemagne's full-fledged endorsement (and mandate) for religious institutions to meet this need.[35] However, Charlemagne institutionalized what had been regional or voluntary among clerics with his *Admonitio Generalis* of A.D. 789. A key part of this, twenty-three paragraphs in section 2, is a call for secular and church leaders to work together, especially in the educational areas of the arts, literature, and law. Another aspect of Charlemagne's mandate pertinent to our study is found in the life and work of Alcuin (d. 804). There was a connection between the gifted cleric and the community, and gifted clerics were generally found associated with a cathedral school.

We could list dozens of popular professors and the flow of students to their rostrums, such as Gerbert of Aurillac, who taught at the Cathedral School at Rheims (972–997).[36] Prosopographic studies validate his popularity by confirming at least twenty-five noted alumni with him (out of forty-one linked through later sources). Those confirmed were in vocations of "bishop and archbishops" (ten), "abbots and monks" (ten), "members of

French and German royal families" (four, including the future Capetian king, Robert the Pious), and "unspecified or lower ranking clerics" (one).[37]

Hugh of St. Victor, cited above, was among the various gifted clerics who factored prominently in the cathedral school movement in Paris. In A.D. 1115, he joined the new Abbey of St. Victor on the bank of the river Seine, and in 1135 he became the master of its school. His *Didascalicon* proved revolutionary—outlining several liberal arts between two groups: the *Trivium* (grammar, logic, and rhetoric) and the *Quadrivium* (arithmetic, music, geometry, and astronomy). Although these are well known in the retelling of education's story, for our discussion look anew at what is being offered. It is a collaboration of a deep sense of contributing to the needs of neighbors, of the state, and of the Church.

The subjects, taught from the context of God the Creator (and Hugh's emphasis on Genesis), would have a twofold purpose. Besides preparation for a profession, through these studies individuals would "produce a life of intellectual and spiritual beauty that mirrored the divine wisdom."[38] As with Peter Abelard, students, who could choose their professors, flocked to his classes. And like Hugh of St. Victor, Abelard also had an important text, *Sic et Non* (foundational for the study of logic), and drew waves of students at his various posts and places before becoming master of Paris' cathedral school at Notre Dame.

Abelard directly competed with others for students and usually won. His main target was his former teacher, William of Champeaux, whom he eventually displaced from Notre Dame. With students choosing and paying the professors of choice, these competitions struck deep and illustrated capitalism on a very public stage. Although the cathedral schools were systematically trying to address the needs of their community while developing their students as being more godly, the numbers of their students often depended on the number of esteemed professors on their rosters.[39]

So as we look at a modern example of collaboration, we bring from the past the threefold notion of being utilitarian, creating a feeder system for society's needs, and relying on gifted faculty (though aware of the challenges). By association with their Christian institution, these faculty are assumed to be theologically charged, with "a well-cultivated appreciation" for their respective religious traditions.[40] In addition, they contend with the complex ways to relate varying identities (such as nationality) and Christianity in the classroom within the boundaries depending on any given institutional setting.[41]

Given our focus on the Christian college, we would do well to heed Russell Moore here on the topic of boundaries. That is, although complexities might arise in merging identities to allow for effective facilitation of what is often called the integration of faith and learning, we also need to be outward looking in terms of what we have learned. He proclaims that "we often forget" that Matthew 5:13–16 (the "salt" and "light" directive) is "imagery that binds together the internal and external witness of the church, the call to both proclamation and demonstration."[42]

Along with the collaboration among cathedral schools in addressing societal needs, we find this balance in Christian professional societies. As of the 2022–2023 academic year, at least forty-two Christian professional societies and ten institutes focused on Christianity and learning.[43] Those associations also support at least eleven discipline-specific Christian journals, with some exceptionally strong reputations such as *Fides et Historia* and *Faith and Philosophy*.[44]

While on some level there is likely overlap between the Christian professional societies and the journals and/or institutes, it is to the formation and function of the societies that we now turn.

In one sense we can make a case that the founding of educating professionals dates back to the cathedral schools, as they were targeting professions such as clerics and accountants—but these were not professions separate from theological moorings or religious affiliations. During the era of cathedral schools, these professional societies were usually tethered in some way to ecclesiastical authority. In the modern era, however, professionals and ultimately their associations separated from nineteenth-century religious educational patterns. This divide arose out of a two-part rejection of the status quo or, in some countries, a disdain for state control. Within the cathedral schools, a more accepting view of classical texts (or pagan writings) had been adopted as the threats on the Church had subsided.[45]

A key part of this professional education came through mentors, such as the Parisian *inception* (literally *to take in hand*, meaning "to begin"). In the Christian college, the internship option is as close as we see to this mentoring model in the professions and is closely aligned with an apprenticeship. In the late nineteenth century, the value of being officially linked through a mentor (beyond today's notion of interning) to a professional association proved invaluable for employment trajectory. "As a consequence, influence within one's professional association soon eclipsed the importance in professional value of a professor's influence on campus."[46]

The forty-plus Christian professional societies and related institutes and journals create a mélange of possibilities today to implement three key components that worked in the cathedral schools. On the utilitarian front, the very gathering of like-minded professionals can identify needs and systems to address them from among member institutions.

As a feeder system for the professional ranks, there are innumerable ways to use Alexander's "open education" model to assist students at all levels in actively working in their guild during college. Perhaps the trickiest is to use dedicated professors within a profession in teaching (or mentoring) the masses. Although the MOOC (massive open online course) model has fallen from the limelight, these professional societies have prominent professors who could play a shared role across institutions.

Collaboration Explored

As with previous chapters, the purpose here is not to propose specific ways to practice collaboration. The vast array of characteristics that define the Christian college make doing so nonsensical. At best, we might be able to propose ways that make sense on one campus but, in turn, distract from efforts being made on all other campuses. As a result, we offer questions concerning collaboration that can inform planning processes ranging from those taking place at the university-wide level to those at the programmatic level.

The logic defining individual and organizational relationships in the contemporary world is one of competition—all too often, competition at all costs. The Christian college, as an extension of the Church's ministry and as a reflection of the world to which we will one day belong, is defined by the web of collaborative relationships. Those relationships and the end to which they are ordered are critical reflections of an understanding of discipleship. When we are in properly ordered relationships, we become aware of our limitations and, in turn, become truly free. That freedom then allows us to grow in character that, in the case of the Christian college, advances our common pursuit of God's truth.

- *What collaborative efforts do senior leaders of the Christian college model between their respective areas on campus? Between their respective areas and comparable areas on other campuses?*

Academic departments are not the only silos or seemingly independent organizational units that define the Christian college. All too often, divisions such as academic affairs, student affairs, admissions, and advancement, to name only four, operate as rivals. Those perceptions of rivalry are often compounded by scarce resources as well as the nature of the personalities leading those units. If senior leaders do not offer tangible examples of collaboration with one another, their subordinates will rarely, if ever, view such an operational logic as a good. Senior leaders are encouraged to detail why collaboration is an extension of discipleship and what lessons it affords community members. Such details, however, will fail to become part of the theological imagination of the community unless they are matched by tangible expressions of action.

- *In what way(s) is the Christian college organized (in terms of its intellectual and organizational architecture) to accomplish collaboration as a vision of discipleship?*

As previously noted, the silo or seemingly independent organizational unit is identified as a source of the challenges plaguing higher education, including the Christian college. Even if senior leaders speak to and model the importance of collaboration on and beyond the campus, the way their organizations are structured may mitigate against their best intentions. Although bureaucracy as an organizational structure has long since been challenged, entities unaccustomed to change, regardless of size, are arguably the most bureaucratic.

On the Christian college campus, for example, one can test the strength of such a cultural sensibility by noting how many faculty members possess dual or courtesy appointments. Are they viewed simply as citizens of one department? Or are they encouraged via various organizational means to share their expertise with broader circles of colleagues and students in useful ways? On an even larger organizational scale, are there units that not only span but also draw together various academic departments? For collaboration to flourish, the intellectual and organizational architecture cannot be allowed to mitigate against it. If anything, the Christian college should be the place that exercises a theological imagination that sees beyond the reductionist impulse that all too often defines how we view truth and, in turn, imposes itself on how we structure institutions.

- *Are curricular units and programs aligned to facilitate collaboration? Are cocurricular units and programs aligned to facilitate collaboration? Are curricular and cocurricular programs and units aligned to facilitate collaboration?*

The two organizational units that have the greatest direct impact on student learning are the curricular and cocurricular. As implied in the previous example concerning curricular units, reductionist ways of pursuing truth forged distinct units, such as biology, and then the myriad subdisciplines grouped beneath them. The question is not whether such subdisciplines should exist and whether faculty and students should be encouraged to reach down within them as far as they can go. The question is whether the same encouragement exists to go across those subdisciplines in an effort to answer a question for which no one subdiscipline houses the resources needed to marshal an answer. To complicate matters, does the same encouragement exist between biology and chemistry, biology and history, or biology and art?

The same is true within cocurricular units, such as residence life, student leadership programs, calling and career programs, campus ministry, multicultural programs, and athletics. Do those units operate as if they are independent of one another? Or are they aligned in such a way that the educators who lead them view the impact of their efforts as being dependent upon the collaborative relationships they share with other units? For example, do athletic coaches view their colleagues in residence life as competitors for student time? Or do they view them as colleagues with whom they collaborate in a larger understanding of discipleship?

The challenges in fostering collaboration between curricular and cocurricular units then proves even more challenging. Too often educators populating those two groups have been socialized toward different educational goods as a result of their graduate training. Even once they wind up serving on the same campus, they rarely work together. Previously posed as a possible challenge among cocurricular educators, competition for student time can produce tension between curricular and cocurricular educators. During tight financial seasons, the two groups can often view each other as competitors for resources. A properly ordered theological imagination, however, views them not as competitors but as participants in a common educational endeavor.

- *What reward structures, if any, encourage individuals and programs to work together?*

No matter how educators serving the Christian college view their work, rewarded efforts may wield more influence than espoused rhetoric. A simple test of such an understanding is the rationale that senior leaders use when highlighting performance. For example, how often are educators in English rewarded for collaborating with colleagues in their department or another department, or with cocurricular educators? At this juncture, one might take a hard look at the criteria used in promotion and tenure review hearings. Are educators in English penalized, or are their efforts valued less when working with others than when working alone?

Consider other ways in which individual performance is highlighted. How often are campus-wide awards given to individuals who worked together? Does an award exist that highlights collaborative efforts made by any number of employees on campus? Senior leaders may want to consider evaluating the reward structures currently in place and also whether new rewards might be useful to reflect the role collaboration plays in the Christian college's understanding of discipleship.

- *In what way(s) are educators on one campus encouraged to collaborate with educators on other campuses? What reward structures, if any, encourage such collaboration?*

Perhaps even greater than the challenge of facilitating collaboration on a campus is facilitating collaboration among campuses. Try as they may, no college or university possesses the fiscal and human resources needed to address the myriad of questions they face today. The Christian college, by virtue of its commitment to discipleship and a properly ordered theological imagination, should reflexively consider how collaboration on and beyond a single campus can be cultivated. By making us aware of our limitations, collaboration fosters the character needed to pursue God's truth as woven into every corner of the created order. That possibility not only exists on a particular campus but also exponentially grows when considering the possibilities that involve other campuses.

Instead of viewing educators serving on other campuses as a threat, collaboration calls for considering them as possible partners in the pursuit of truth. How does the rhetoric employed on the campus encourage or discourage such relationships? Do senior leaders speak of sister institutions as partners in a common endeavor? Or do they speak of their peers at those institutions and/or those individuals in a derisive manner? Such references set the tone for what colleagues deem socially permissible.

In addition, what reward structures, if any, may encourage such collaboration? Assuming the language employed on campus cultivates the perception that collaboration is socially permissible, do the reward structures in place reinforce or undercut that understanding? Such structures can be as formal as campus awards and details in place in promotion and tenure requirements. Informal structures might include achievements that get noted in public meetings as well as on institutional websites and social media platforms; these affirmations often speak volumes about whether such efforts are valued.

* * *

As highlighted by Dietrich Bonhoeffer, the question God posed to Gideon when facing the Midianites was not whether Gideon was to collaborate with others but with whom he was to collaborate. First, God wanted Gideon to know that God was by Gideon's side. Any praise that was to come from a victory against such an overpowering force was to be offered to God, for only God's grace was sufficient. Second, Gideon was called to stand with others on that day, though not with the army Gideon originally sought to summon. As Bonhoeffer would highlight in *Creation and Fall*, the collaborative relationships that God called Gideon to forge allowed Gideon and his fellow warriors to lean on God and one another out of the stark realization that they depended upon one another. Such a realization then becomes the ground out of which character grows.

By virtue of its history, the culture in which it exists, and the way its reward structures are often detailed and communicated, collaboration amid the Christian-college milieu is arguably in short supply. More often than not, campuses depend upon themselves with organizational units and individual educators following suit in their respective areas of responsibility. Bonhoeffer poses a challenge to that logic, arguing that collaboration is an expression of an understanding of discipleship defined by a properly ordered theological imagination.

4

Illumination

Despite his concerns about the threats posed to Germany and regions beyond by the rise of the National Socialist Party, even Dietrich Bonhoeffer was incapable of imagining the full weight of the prophetic words he uttered from the pulpit of Berlin's Trinity Church on Sunday, February 26, 1933.

Earlier that month, members of the National Socialist Party began making frequent requests to hold rallies across Germany in churches as well as in marketplaces and on university campuses. To some clergy, such requests came as welcomed signs: the revival Germany so desperately needed was not simply political and economic but also spiritual.

For example, Joachim Hossenfelder, a leader to German Christians and the author of "The Original Guidelines of the German Christian Faith Movement," argued in 1932 that churches were vital parts of the revival the National Socialist Party sought to initiate.[1] Guideline 5 reads:

> We want to bring to our church the reawakened German sense of life and to revitalize our church. In the fateful struggle for German freedom and our future, the leadership of the church has proven to be too weak. Up to this point the

church has not risen to the challenge of a determined struggle against godless Marxism and the Center Party, so alien
to our spirit; instead, it has made a compact with the political parties of these powers. We want our church to be front
and center in the battle that will decide the life or death of
our people. The church may not stand on the sidelines or
dissociate itself from those who are fighting for freedom.[2]

Guideline 9 then includes these tragic words:

In the mission to the Jews we see great danger to our people. It is the point at which foreign blood enters the body of
our people. There is no justification for its existing alongside the foreign mission. We reject the mission to the Jews
as long as Jews have citizenship, which brings with it the
danger of raceblurring and race-bastardizing. Holy Scripture speaks both of holy wrath and of self-denying love. It
is especially important to prohibit marriages between Germans and Jews.[3]

Despite those grave accommodations, Hossenfelder's relationship
with the National Socialist Party proved short-lived. On November 29, 1933, the *New York Times* reported, "REICH FORCES
OUT CHURCH EXTREMIST; Hossenfelder, Leader of Nazi German Christians, Quits the Protestant Governing Body."[4]

The day after Bonhoeffer offered his sermon on Judges 6:15–16;
7:2; 8:23 to the congregation gathered at Berlin's Trinity Church,
the Reichstag, the home of Germany's parliament, burned,
reportedly the target of arson. Originally decried as a Communist crime, the Nazis blamed the act on "a half-witted Dutch
Communist with a passion for arson Marinus van der Lubbe."[5]
Historians, in contrast, believe that "the idea for the fire almost
certainly originated with [Joseph] Goebbels and [Herman Wil-
helm] Goering"[6]—eventually Hitler's chief propagandist and
commander of the Luftwaffe, respectively.

On that Tuesday, Hitler capitalized on the fear initiated by the Reichstag's burning, persuading President Hindenburg to issue a decree designed to protect the people and the state by suspending "seven sections of the constitution which guaranteed individual and civil liberties."[7] Among others, those freedoms included speech and association. The state was also granted the right to monitor communication and issue search warrants without the previous burdens of demonstrating cause.

For congregants who would wander into such realities over the course of the next forty-eight hours, Bonhoeffer spent no time in his sermon on that Sunday on the details of Gideon's conquest. Most, if not all, who joined Bonhoeffer on that morning knew Gideon was victorious in battle. What Bonhoeffer wanted them to know was to whom and to what end Gideon attributed that victory. With these points in mind, Bonhoeffer asked, how can they be confounded by the Gideons among them "who see in the midst of our church the cross, which is the sign of powerlessness, dishonor, defenselessness, hopelessness, meaninglessness, and yet is also where we find divine power, honor, defense, hope, meaning, glory, life, and victory?"[8] Drawn by faith, Bonhoeffer wanted them to "see the direct line from Gideon to the cross."[9]

With the tide of human pretension rising right outside the church door on that Sunday morning, the ability of congregants to follow that line would mean God alone deserves the victory on that day. The cross of Christ stands as a testament not only to "God's lordship over all the world" but also to "God's bitter suffering in all human misery."[10] No matter what end of a spectrum may be dominating human existence during a particular season, God is present in full amid all of creation. Bonhoeffer likely knew on that Sunday that the Church would need to choose between two options. It might follow Joachim Hossenfelder's lead and exercise the force of its will, regardless of complicit collaborations: "want[ing] our church to be front and center in the battle that will decide the life or death of our people." Or the Church might assume that God would abandon them in what could become a season of "human misery." Neither form of thinking would reflect a third option: "the direct line from Gideon to the cross."

Amid that rising tide of human pretension, Bonhoeffer also wanted congregants who heard these words from Judges to remember to what end credit was due when it came to the victory Gideon and his army experienced on that day. By faith, Gideon and his army experienced the victory God afforded them. As with all details in life, they were called to glorify God. They were, in fact, to celebrate their victory and speak of the faithfulness of God who delivered them. The question is not whether they were to speak of their victory but rather to what end they were to speak of it. Were they to speak of it as a reflection of their own might? Or were they to speak of it as a way of bearing witness to the only light that can illuminate even the darkest corners of the world? Only the latter would prove to be a proper expression of the end to which they attributed that victory. As Germany under the rule of the Nazis ominously became one of the darkest corners of the world in human history, remembering to what end the Church was to share the light of faith would grow more critical.

Bonhoeffer closes his sermon on that day by noting what may be Gideon's greatest moment. That moment was not when he led his army into battle. Nor was it when that army proved victorious. That moment was when the Israelites came to Gideon, now victorious in battle, and presented him with what Bonhoeffer called "the final trial. The final temptation."[11] In particular, they asked Gideon in that moment if he would rule over them.

History is tragically littered with people who could not walk away from such temptations of power—temptations that present themselves at the most inopportune moments—when such individuals were at the zeniths of influence. Gideon, however, had "not forgotten his own history, nor this history of his people."[12] His greatest moment was thus when he reminded them that God and God alone would rule over them. Echoing the first commandment given to Moses, Gideon declared that "you shall have no other gods" (Exod 20:3 [RSV]). His greatest moment

was when the light he was called to bear was the light of faith
only God could give.

* * *

Now Adam knew Eve his wife, and she conceived and bore
Cain, saying, "I have gotten a man with the help of the LORD."
And again, she bore his brother Abel. Now Abel was a keeper
of sheep, and Cain a tiller of the ground. In the course of
time Cain brought to the LORD an offering of the fruit of the
ground, and Abel brought of the firstlings of his flock and of
their fat portions. And the LORD had regard for Abel and his
offering, but for Cain and his offering he had no regard. So
Cain was very angry, and his countenance fell.
—Genesis 4:1–5 (RSV)

Perhaps the component of the planning process most foreign
to the Christian college is illumination. After discerning what
understanding of discipleship orders its imagination and animates efforts of collaboration, the Christian college, whether it
does so at the institutional level or the programmatic level, needs
to consider how it shares its message. A cursory review of a variety of institutional webpages reveals little to no strategic thinking
in terms of the narrative being deployed. Although the messages
and images may be different, a safe argument is that such efforts
barely exceed the organizational efforts the average individual
invests into a TikTok, Instagram, Twitter, or Facebook account.
Information seems to relay what was readily available, reflective
of no larger narrative or purpose, and arranged as clickbait for
audiences primarily if not singularly composed of prospective
students. Many reasons behind such narrow efforts at illumination exist, but we will consider three.

First, the chief information officer on many campuses may
also be the chief student enrollment officer. The success or failure of that person is measured by the single criterion of meeting
an enrollment target. In an age of fierce competition for students

among many campuses, doubling down on communications with prospective students, while understandable, is unfortunate. One may meet an enrollment goal one year but have done so at the expense of an opportunity to build an appreciation for a message among an audience of which prospective students are but one sector. In addition, prospective students across generations are attracted to a compelling message and identity, not fleeting efforts at appeal.

Second, many campuses do not have a history and culture known for being invested in efforts of illumination reflective of a well-crafted, multilayered, nuanced, and theologically grounded message. Qualified personnel are often difficult to find and come with considerable expense. In previous years, the voice of a university president through readily available messaging media may have proven sufficient. Today few university presidents are viewed as public intellectuals whose reputations can embody the messages of the campuses they represent. Even the most widely recognized and erudite leaders today need assistance in crafting messages their respective institutions are called to illuminate.

Third, many campuses do not think, in their most honest moments, that they have anything to offer in terms of a messaging effort. Whatever pride employees may have on their own campus may quickly fade when they find themselves in communication with constituents near or far from home. Justification for that proposed challenge is readily offered by any employee who starts a sentence with the phrase, "We're a small school." In higher education, better is not bigger. Better is better. Such a phrase is arguably a cover for low institutional self-esteem and, in turn, an excuse to avoid responsibility for grappling with the questions, to whom and to what end are they called to serve as agents of illumination?

As argued in previous chapters, the sermon that Bonhoeffer shared with congregants gathered in Berlin's Trinity Church on Sunday, February 26, 1933, is rooted in his theological exegesis of Genesis 1–4:1 as found in *Creation and Fall*. Bonhoeffer notes that as a result of Adam and Eve's decision to eat from the tree of life—the one decision God prohibited them from making—Adam and Eve and all of their descendants would live in a world "between God's curse and promise."[13] Such a world is defined by the disorienting yet present reality concerning the relationship that the knowledge of pain and the knowledge of pleasure share with each other. Childbirth, despite the pleasure it yields when the eyes of a parent and the eyes of a child meet for the first time, now also yields great pain. Work, despite the pleasure it yields when one's talents are exercised well, now also yields great pain.

When living in the anxious middle between curse and promise, the pleasures these experiences yield find their fulfillment this side of eternity when humanity grapples rightly with the questions of to whom and to what end credit is properly given. Bonhoeffer's theological exegesis of Genesis 1–4:1 ends with an exploration of how Adam and Eve's descendant Cain grappled with this question. Bonhoeffer's interest in Cain and in his story is because "Cain is the first human being who is born on the ground that is *cursed*. It is with Cain that history begins, the history of death."[14]

In Cain, Bonhoeffer finds one who defies that "only the Creator can destroy life. Cain usurps for himself this ultimate right of the Creator and becomes the murderer."[15] Cain takes the life of his brother, Abel, the second human being who is born on the ground that is cursed. At the conclusion of *Creation and Fall*, Bonhoeffer focuses on the gravity of Cain's sin in Cain's desire to take upon himself a role that solely belonged to God. For our purposes, it will prove necessary to explore not only why Bonhoeffer theologically explains why Cain made that choice but also how that choice differs from the one Abel made; that is, to whom and to what end did they offer their respective gifts?

Bonhoeffer understandably ends his effort with a theological exploration of Cain's choice to take his brother's life. Bonhoeffer believes that "the end of Cain's history, and so the end of all history, is Christ on the cross, the murdered Son of God."[16] Bonhoeffer views Cain as making one final, tragic move to reverse the fateful decision made by his parents. If he, in fact, controlled his own life and could reenter paradise, he would prove humans possessed the power the Serpent proclaimed to Eve and, in turn, Adam. The gate that God sealed behind Adam and Eve when God expelled them from paradise remains closed. They will live between pleasure and pain, in the anxious middle, until the "accursed ground" upon which they are called to walk, the lives they are called to lead, are "raised up anew," not by a return to the wood of the tree of life but by the "wood of the cross."[17]

Cain's sin, while tragically confirmed by his willingness to take the life of his brother, Abel, rests in his inability to recognize to whom and to what end he was to offer the fruits of his labor. Cain, as "a tiller of the ground," offered to God what Cain desired, not what God desired. Cain brought "the fruit of the ground," but God desired the "firstlings of his flock and of their fat portions." God had no regard for Cain's offering. At this point, Cain's motivation to act on his desires becomes most apparent. He becomes "very angry, his countenance fell," and he makes a desperate attempt at validating his desires by taking Abel's life. The end of Cain's sacrifice, the fruit of the ground, was about not God's glorification but his own. As is so often the case with human motivation, the question of to whom such a gift was offered inevitably curves back and points to Cain, not to God.

In contrast to Cain, the gift Abel offers is for God and God's glorification. He offers what is pleasing and glorifying to God, not to himself. Cain's anger tragically confirms Abel's sacrifice and the illumination it offers. Cain is incapable of seeing beyond himself and offering praise and honor to anyone else. Abel's answers to the questions concerning to whom and to what end his sacrifice is to be offered only enrages Cain. Abel, like Gideon, has no other gods including the most tempting of all gods to worship—himself.

Bonhoeffer and the congregants who gathered with him in Berlin's Trinity Church on that Sunday in February 1933 would also come to learn the importance of bearing witness to a God who illuminated the earth through the sacrifice of Jesus Christ and the ongoing presence of the Holy Spirit.

As technology provides the Christian college with more means each day of participating in that calling of illumination, the underlying questions remain the same—to whom and to what end is such illumination offered?

Illumination Exemplified

We have witnessed various revolutions in education. There are three according to Vishal Mangalwadi, known for *This Book Changed Everything*. His more recent book is aptly titled *The Third Education Revolution: Home School to Church College*.[18]

The first revolution in his outline is the Carolingian Renaissance of the eighth and ninth centuries. The Church educated clergy to minister in both the Church and the state (thus various countries still have prime ministers, at least in name). The second revolution in education was the democratization of knowledge and governance following Martin's Luther's challenge for the Church to educate everyone to be "priest and king" (*Open Letter to the Nobility of the German Nation*, 1520). Mangalwadi's third revolution is a projection, proposed to occur when the whole system flips. That is, instead of the Church sending students to universities, the universities will start sending students to the Church. Although the first two revolutions indeed occurred, the last is up for debate (not its conceptual merit, but actualization on a larger scale).[19]

We pause here to look at the genesis of what Mangalwadi terms the second educational revolution associated with the Reformation. While we often cite movable type and Johannes Gutenberg's printing press as being among the most important inventions in history, we should also list it among the most revolutionary forces on education at all levels. Diarmaid MacCulloch categorizes the printing press as being among "the great populist weapons of the sixteenth-century Reformation" along with "hymns and songs."[20] By 1500, fewer than fifty years after that first batch of 185 Bibles was printed, there were books in some twenty languages. By the early 1500s, approximately a thousand print shops surfaced in various parts of Europe and, by 1539, appeared in Mexico City. This development offers us a backdrop to think of its dynamics in the light of illumination. How are the Christian college and its educators giving their talents unto God? In addition, in some shared space with other institutions? The late medieval example below developed into illumination as the Reformers channeled it toward ministry ends, but Gutenberg's journey is ripe with lessons for our current discussion.

By 1454/1455, Gutenberg had launched a revolution. He perfected his book's pages for reading ease (the old two-column manuscript layout with forty to forty-two lines), printed on thicker, damp paper for the ink to bond and not smear, and made it possible to employ the revolutionary linseed oil and lampblack ink. He also chose the black letter gothic type font (to look like the manuscripts). Relocating twice was part of his journey while he explored options that would work. His presses even came to apply just the right pressure to the page.[21]

The other part of his story, however, is not as positive—the financial pressure. Gutenberg had a promising and brilliant idea. As the pages were still drying on his now priceless Bibles, he felt pressure from his creditor, Mainz businessman Johann Fust. According to one account, Gutenberg died poor and marginalized when Fust called in his loans and took credit for Gutenberg's invention. Gutenberg's understudy, Peter Schöffer, testified against his printing mentor in court, partnered with Fust, and became wealthy.[22] The majority of Schöffer's early books were religious, and in 1565 he even counterfeited Johannes Mentelin's copy of St. Augustine's *De arte praedicandi* (*The Art of Preaching*). While little consolation, Gutenberg's fame was restored posthumously.

Movable type transformed (or revolutionized) education when it gained wider access beyond a single printed Bible costing the price of some homes. "Printing technology contributed to the opening of the European mind only after the Protestant Reformation made God's Word affordable for the common person in his mother-tongue. Studying God's Word demystified religion. As people sought truth, they were able to question human authority, enslaving superstitions and myths."[23]

Books would also transform the university classroom. Perhaps three classroom staples existed at the end of the fifteenth century as printing was still finding outlets. Parisian Bibles in manuscript form were uniform in both their text and layout—and rather portable in pocket Bible size (far less expensive than the great Bibles, though not cheap).[24] A second staple was the wax tablet for copying texts that the professor read aloud from a precious copy of a great text (on vellum or parchment). The third staple was the professor—and one's reputation often determined the class size and income.

Printed books, however, radically changed these staples by the mid-1550s. The entire industry for producing wax tablets waned. Students had access to actual texts, though many were chained in their libraries (like on display in the Hereford Cathedral and the Sackler Library in Oxford). Others were student copies with large margins (and filled with years of other students' notes).[25] Regardless, students had direct access to a wider array of thinkers and more time to digest the insights and information. Around 1590, Rabbi Jacob ben Isaac Ashkenazi, for example, reflected on this dynamic with printed texts: "They speak too rapidly in the synagogue, but in this book one can read slowly, so that he himself will understand."[26]

As universities proliferated, so did university presses—but, curiously, only decades later. Cambridge University Press published its first book in 1584,[27] claiming to be the oldest university press. Oxford University Press followed in 1586. Note that both came a century after the printing of Gutenberg's Bible. One mitigating factor: the major manuscript production was in cities with universities because of the dependence on scholars as advisers and editors.

Very early—this is true especially in Italy—we find scholars serving as advisers and correctors to the printers. It is only natural, therefore, that the copyists, who belonged to the stationers' gilds, which were especially strong in university towns, should have fought against the introduction of printing. Nowhere in Germany with the possible exception of Cologne, nor in Basel, nor in Italy, did there exist any connection between early presses and the universities.[28]

In the modern era, an example of illumination is found in the University of Notre Dame's award-winning "What Would You Fight For?" series along with its FaithND and ThinkND programs for alumni and friends of the university. Whereas former president Theodore M. Hesburgh, C.S.C., did not want reporters asking questions about the storied football program every time they called (and he would refer them to the athletic director), his successors realized the value of endorsing this beloved team. The question "What Would You Fight For?" is immediately recognizable to the hundreds of millions who have watched the TV spots. Notre Dame claims:

> The series showcases the work, scholarly achievements, and global impact of Notre Dame faculty, students, and alumni. These two-minute segments, each originally aired during a home football game broadcast on NBC, highlight the University's proud moniker, the Fighting Irish, and tell the stories of the members of the Notre Dame family who fight to bring solutions to a world in need.[29]

Each of the titles magnifies this stated mission and offers a prime example of illumination. "Fighting to Educate a Different Kind of Lawyer" is an admirable reflection of its program in which "law students represent disabled clients scammed out of their benefits in the largest Social Security fraud in U.S. history." It is an engaging and heartwarming segment of Notre Dame students giving invaluable help to once destitute Appalachians in or near the impoverished town of Prestonsburg, Kentucky. It prompts hope in the American college system and especially in Notre Dame.

This series has gone to some of the largest NBC viewing audiences for nearly two decades. In 2020, Notre Dame football games established the mark of the highest viewership in fifteen years for five games, "a Total Audience Delivery (TAD) of 4.802 million viewers, marking the most-watched season on NBC since 2005 (5.168 million P2+)."[30] All of the "Fight For" titles have this outward-looking feel: "Fighting for Technology That Saves Lives"; "Fighting for Clean Water"; and "Fighting to Bring Literacy to the World."

The authors interviewed Beth Grisoli, Notre Dame's director of multimedia services. We learned that the vice president of the Office of Public Affairs and Communications signs off on the messaging before it goes public. "As long as we have stories of impact to share," she offered, "we plan to continue the series." The following are some of the other parts of this exchange from August 5, 2022:

- *When did the "What Would You Fight For?" campaign begin, and what is the basic historic narrative?*

The series began in 2007. When NBC and Notre Dame finalized their football broadcast contract, Notre Dame mentioned to NBC that it would be wonderful to share some of the great academic and research endeavors of Notre Dame to remind viewers of our true mission as a university. Thus, the concept of the 2:00 stories at the end of halftime was born.

- *The series is among the best examples of all universities today with a discernible message. If you were to give other institutions of higher education a recipe for such messaging, what would be its key ingredients? In addition, were these present from the first episode? If not, how have they changed?*

We have stayed consistent in our messaging goals from the outset. We try to showcase the true breadth and depth of Notre

Dame—a global research institution committed to exceptional undergraduate education, informed by a deep and rich faith tradition. We aspire to transform people's lives: (1) our students' lives through education and service; (2) our faculty members' lives through their pursuit of truth; and (3) the lives of those around the world through our work. I would suggest other institutions hone in on their individual missions and priorities and focus on communicating the reasons behind those particular priorities. If you decide to share stories to illustrate your mission in action, make sure they are authentic and not contrived. Look for stories that will connect with your audience's humanity.

- *The series weds various disciplines with the audience recognition of Notre Dame's athletic mantra. Was there a key development that helped the academic and athletic sides come together? What advice do you have for leaders to recognize the benefits of wedding academics with an area of extracurricular success?*

I referenced our conversations with NBC a bit in question 1. That was a significant moment, I believe. We don't put football front and center, but it happens to draw a very large audience for us. We see the value in a captive audience and set out to educate viewers that our university amounts to much more than Saturday football games. I would encourage any university or college to make use of an audience they have established to share university messaging. Even if people are there for a conference, a convention, or recreation, why not make use of the opportunity?

- *Dietrich Bonhoeffer highlights the need for gifts and services to be unto God rather than self. What has been the process in selecting individuals representing this aspect of the series? What is the theme that reflects the priority of Christian heritage and divine purpose in the highlighted careers of the episodes?*

The theme harks back to our roots in the Congregation of Holy Cross [the university's founding religious order]: Fr. Basil Moreau, C.S.C., said, "The mind will not be cultivated at the expense of the heart. While we prepare useful citizens for society, we shall likewise do our utmost to prepare citizens for heaven." He preached, "Education is helping a young person to be more like Christ, the model of all Christians." Every discipline of study or research at Notre Dame has this purpose.

We select individuals for the "What Would You Fight For?" series based on the quality of their academic and/or research endeavors and how those efforts support the greater good. The subject matter also needs to be relatable to the average person.

- *How does ND evaluate the return on investment on this series?*

We don't do any formal return on investment reports, but we monitor NBC's rating information and online analytics for the stories' individual webpages and our posts on Twitter, Instagram, and Facebook.

- *Is the series asking for a response of its viewers? If so, what?*

We pose the question with that hope that everyone will consider an answer and be inspired to work toward that goal, and in doing so each may become more like Christ.

Inspiration for how one can become more like Christ as an extension of what they would fight for does not end with the stories highlighted by this series. In recent years, the University of Notre Dame Alumni Association (with its mission of strengthening the bonds of alumni, parents, and friends "to Notre Dame and each other; help[ing] them thrive in faith, service, learning, and work; and inspir[ing] them to act as forces for good in their communities and the world")[31] developed two new online programs—FaithND and ThinkND. No matter where people may be at a given time and location, an internet connection allows them to participate in ongoing formation on a daily basis as informed by the university's resources.

FaithND, for example, extends an invitation to all interested persons to participate in any number of daily experiences designed to nurture their faith as inspired by the university's

Catholic and Holy Cross mission. Those experiences include the opportunity to share prayer requests that volunteers offer at the Grotto on campus, watch Mass from the campus' Basilica of the Sacred Heart Monday through Friday, and listen to episodes from the *Everyday Holiness* podcast series.

For example, the most recent episode in that podcast series at the time of writing is with Bishop William A. Wack, C.S.C., a Notre Dame graduate and Congregation of Holy Cross priest who began his service as bishop of the Diocese of Pensacola-Tallahassee in 2017. In that episode, Bishop Bill talked about his own faith journey, his call to ministry, and his commitment to serve the Church as a member of its episcopate.[32]

Perhaps the most widely recognizable and used component of the FaithND program is the Daily Gospel Reflection delivered via email. Established in 2013, these reflections include four components: the daily Gospel reading from the lectionary; a devotional reflecting on the reading offered by a member of the Notre Dame community (most often alumni, but also administrators, faculty members, parents of current students, and current students); a prayer offered by a member of the Congregation of Holy Cross; and a brief biography of the saint of the day. The amount of time participants take to reflect upon and pray over the content varies widely. Reading the content each day takes approximately fifteen minutes.

For example, the Gospel reading for Thursday, September 29, 2022, was John 1:47–51. Often referenced as Nathanael's encounter with Jesus, this passage includes Christ's admonishment: "Here is a true child of Israel. There is no duplicity in him." The passage, however, concludes with Jesus addressing Nathanael: "Amen, amen, I say to you, you will see heaven opened and the angels of God ascending and descending on the Son of Man." The reflection, offered by Notre Dame alumna and employee Carolyn Pirtle, focuses on what we can learn from Nathanael and what it means to see such great things. Being absent duplicity like Nathanael, Pirtle writes, "are the ones who will, one day, behold the Son of

Man in his glory and will worship him in the presence not only of the archangels but of all the angels and the saints, singing before the throne of God forever."[33] The prayer was offered by M. Joseph Pederson, C.S.C., and the short biography of the saint of the day was of Sts. Michael, Gabriel, and Raphael—appropriately on the archangels' feast day according to the Church calendar.

While the ThinkND platform includes content reflective of the university's commitment to foster the relationship shared by faith and learning, its formal focus is to provide "free online learning opportunities from across the University." To do so, ThinkND offers those opportunities through articles, podcast series, videos, and virtual events delivered through platforms such as Zoom. To share details concerning new and upcoming events, an email digest is sent each Sunday morning. Visitors to the website can also search the ever-expanding volume of content, for example, by topic, college or school, and name.

For example, on Tuesday, September 27, 2022, the School of Architecture hosted "Notre-Dame de Paris: Architecting a Legacy" with Philippe Villeneuve and Rémi Fromont, the architects leading the effort to reconstruct the cathedral. In particular, they spoke "about the cathedral's devastating fire in 2019 and their restoration efforts, progress, and plans."[34] Individuals could attend the event in person or virtually via Zoom and the ThinkND program.

Although the use of available forms of technology—whether the printing press or internet-based programs—is beneficial, the critical issue at hand is: What messages are university communities seeking to share? Do they have a sense of their respective messages? Have they developed those messages in nuanced ways that reach various segments of their audiences? And, perhaps most critically, do they believe they have a message worthy of sharing?

By virtue of being birthed by the Church, the answer, at least to that last question, should prove obvious to the Christian college. While it anticipates the world in which it belongs, aspiration, imagination, and collaboration offer the Christian college a message capable of illuminating even the world's darkest corners.

Illumination Explored

Illumination is the final stage in a planning process designed to aid the Christian college in fulfilling its calling while navigating the anxious middle between God's curse and promise. Such a process is designed to be used on any number of levels, ranging from the programmatic to the institutional. Such a process, however, must include the consideration of all three of the previously noted steps. Depending upon their respective missions, organizational structures, and geographical locations, colleges and universities may want to consider adding other steps to the process.

Whatever process emerges, it must be defined by an understanding of what aspiration for discipleship animates its social imagination that, in turn, determines how collaboration and illumination are exercised. Assuming the participants in a planning process have invested the needed energy into those matters, below please find some questions to aid in the development of a message the Christian college is called to illuminate.

- *Does the Christian college have a discernible messaging effort? If so, how is the messaging effort an extension of its understanding of discipleship?*

As noted earlier in this chapter, a discernible messaging effort on the part of the Christian college is difficult to identify via a review of websites along with related social media accounts found on platforms such as Instagram, Facebook, and Twitter. On a theological level, such confusion is an inexcusable exercise of the mission to which the Christian college is called. Wesleyan, Reformed, Baptist, and nondenominational institutions, to name only four traditions, should approach these questions in ways that reflect their own theological heritages and how those heritages inform discipleship. Regardless, the particularities those heritages generate need to be discernible and then prayerfully nuanced in such a way that they animate an entity as complex as the Christian college.

On a practical level, such articulation is critical if the Christian college is going to illuminate a world in need with its message.

Woven into the details, regardless of the particularities of the message, should reside its understanding of discipleship. The institution as a whole, of course, needs to reflect such an understanding in its messaging and the calendar it follows when deploying that message. All subunits, whether they be divisions, departments, or programs, need to reflect in their own nuanced ways how such an understanding of discipleship animates their efforts. As a result, the Christian college's messaging efforts and the calendars that structure their messages should reflect a sense of unity forged by a common commitment without being uniform or canned in delivery.

- *With what audience(s) is the Christian college poised to share that message? What messaging strategy coordinates such efforts?*

If an understanding of discipleship resides at the core of all messaging efforts, the next critical concern the Christian college (and the entities that comprise it) needs to consider is this: With whom are they striving to share that message? As previously noted, a review of webpages and related social media accounts leaves one to think the only audience with whom the Christian college is striving to communicate is prospective students and individuals who influence their decisions. Prospective students are certainly important. However, they are but one of several important audiences that should also include, for example, Church leaders and members, foundation leaders, business leaders, policymakers, journalists, artists, prospective donors, and alumni.

For example, when viewing the webpage for a political science department, would a journalist know who is available for comment concerning a particular matter? Is it clear to a foundation looking to invest its resources that the department demonstrates a desire to be a resource to local, state, national, and international audiences? Is it clear to prospective students who will teach their classes and what expertise educators bring to bear in those contexts? When students or alumni apply for graduate and professional school, is the quality of education received clear to individuals reviewing reference letters?

Again, the faculty and staff members who populate an academic department should not be left to create and deploy a message on their own. They need the guidance that a dean, provost, and chief information officer can offer when developing such a message along with a calendar detailing its deployment. The result should be a messaging effort that clearly reflects the role they play on and beyond the campus and the expertise they continually seek to cultivate and advance. Such an effort, however, should also reflect the Christian college's larger aspiration for discipleship. On a more mundane level, it should also fit within the institution's larger message calendar as well as honor the institution's branding scheme via the employment of colors, fonts, and logos.

- *How are members of the community invited to participate in those efforts? What forms of professional development prepare those members to participate?*

Messaging will succumb to the temptation of uniformity unless community members are prepared to be informed, active participants in the process. A chief information officer as well as other senior officials on campus need to lead those efforts while providing their colleagues with the resources necessary to participate in what then will be a nuanced yet unified effort. The Christian college needs to be aware of all of its stakeholders and potential audiences. It then needs to engage any number of divisions, departments, and programs that will uniquely contribute to campaigns to reach that audience. For example, the university needs to engage with its business department faculty as well as cocurricular educators in its calling and career office when devising ways to cultivate relationships with corporations. Those corporations then need to be part of the ongoing and expanding set of constituents with whom they interact.

Chief information officers and their colleagues need to provide ongoing training for educators across the campus, addressing how to identify respective audiences and then devising and deploying strategies for reaching them. As divisions, departments, programs, and individuals, educators should be expected to leverage their training as an ongoing part of their professional contributions. A planning process provides a prime opportunity to reach out to new audiences and expand their messaging efforts in new and different ways.

Such training also provides chief information officers and their colleagues with opportunities to open up lines of communication with educators. When educators have breakthroughs or stories that contribute to their division, department, or program's messaging strategy, they will know whom to contact to propose that it might be useful to the university's larger messaging strategy. When a crisis occurs, they will also have reasonable expectations about one another's roles and how they can best work together.

- *When a crisis occurs, how is the Christian college prepared to respond? As an extension of its understanding of discipleship? When that crisis passes, in what way(s) and with what speed does it return to its message?*

The Christian college is not immune to crises. Given the expectations its constituents have for its mission, crises often can—and sometimes perhaps should—take on a greater moral weight for the Christian (rather than secular) college. The question, however, is not whether a crisis will occur; the question is, in such a situation, how does the Christian college's messaging inform its response? Although the particularities of a crisis may come as a surprise, their possibility should not. The Christian college's messaging efforts on any number of levels should be ready to roll out to address almost any challenge.

Given the possibility of greater moral weight being attached to a crisis, perhaps an important test of the strength of an institution's discipleship efforts comes during such moments. Does the Christian college respond in a way that uniquely reflects those lessons? Or does it simply respond in a way a secular institution may via its crisis management functions? A crisis is a test—however undesirable—of an aspiration of discipleship. In those moments, the Christian college may learn more about the strengths of such an aspiration and, when time allows, learn what it can about its strengths and weaknesses.

Although a crisis may be an important component of the Christian college's messaging effort at a particular point in time, that unsettled season should be as short as functionally necessary, being respectful of the individuals directly impacted. The Christian college's default messaging effort should be determined by its message calendar, not by ad hoc responses to positive or negative circumstances. In such moments, sensitivity and discipline are needed, as the Christian college navigates how and when it may return to its planned, scheduled messaging efforts.

* * *

In the current season of life in the anxious middle, the shadows emanating from the darkness that typically shrouds the world's darkest corners threaten to envelop all sectors of society. The Christian college cannot ignore the challenges those shadows pose. The question, as a result, is not whether the Christian college will respond but how the Christian college will respond. The temptation is great to confuse to whom and to what end that response is oriented. The temptation Gideon faced to usurp God's place in the lives of his people was one he faced in victory. Perhaps that temptation is even greater, however, when fear permeates the culture. Will the Christian college and the individuals who lead it succumb to that fear and issue a message, like Cain, that invariably curves in on themselves? Or will they serve as a means of illumination that bears the light of faith only God could give? Only the latter is a light powerful enough to turn back the shadows cast by an advancing darkness.

Even during seasons when those shadows are short, the Church that gave birth to the Christian college still yearns for the world in which it will belong. The Christian college's aspiration for discipleship animates its social imagination that then, in turn, determines how collaboration and illumination are exercised in hope on the shores of Babylon.

Postscript 1

Jon S. Kulaga
Indiana Wesleyan University President

Reflecting on the "salt" shared within the cover of *The Anxious Middle*, I had two simultaneous, yet different, reactions. One micro, the other macro. One temporal, one eternal.

Reading through each chapter, my immediate impression was the micro application these chapters have for my own university. At Indiana Wesleyan University, we have three robust higher education enterprises functioning under the same university: a traditional residential campus of almost 2,500 students; a national online presence with around 8,200 students; and a seminary approaching 600 students. With such vibrant entities coexisting in such proximity to one another, one would think that collaborating would be our lifeblood and strategic advantage.

However, what I have discovered in my short tenure to date as president is we are more willing to collaborate with outside entities that are a mission-fit rather than with ourselves. As each entity watches "their" budget and "their" enrollment to see if "their" staff" and "their" faculty" will be impacted, the larger perspective of the university is lost. It is easy to watch over the condition of one's own silo and still lose sight of the farm.

Another "micro" element Ream and Pattengale emphasize is discipleship with the clarion call to make it happen everywhere.

Discipleship should not be the raison d'être of the religion faculty or the chaplain's office alone. Such a shared responsibility is, fortunately, happening at Indiana Wesleyan University and is seen everywhere from the residence halls to the athletic fields. For example, in fall 2022 over 1,200 students participated in over 190 small groups, with students being discipled and mentored in a host of intentional ways. Marching band members are being led to Christ and baptized in the recreational center pool. Students are being led to Christ in our general education New Testament classes, and our men's basketball program leads our athletic department's spiritual formation strategy with Head Coach Greg Tonagel's "I AM THIRD" program and Assistant Coach Jeff Clark's "Praying On Offense" initiatives. Yes, discipleship can happen everywhere, but rare is the place where it actually happens intentionally, or extensively.

But what came to mind after reading the four chapters—Aspiration, Imagination, Collaboration, and Illumination—was the idea of perhaps a fifth chapter. Sometimes, what is implied needs to be made explicit. So, my imaginary fifth chapter would be titled Incarnation. In *Creation and Fall*, as well as his other works, Bonhoeffer makes it clear that Christ is the end.

In writing about Genesis 3:21 and under the heading "God's New Action," Bonhoeffer writes:

> Adam's life, as we have already pointed out, is preserved until it finds its end in death; our life is preserved only until it finds its end in—Christ. All orders of our fallen world are God's orders of preservation that uphold and preserve us for Christ. They are not orders of creation but orders of preservation. They have no value in themselves; instead, they find their end and meaning only through Christ.

A few years later in 1937, Bonhoeffer would write *The Cost of Discipleship*, describing the call to discipleship as "nothing else than bondage to Jesus Christ alone, completely breaking through every programme. . . . No other significance is possible, since Jesus is the only significance. . . . He alone matters" (p. 63).

Which leads me to my hypothetical fifth chapter, Incarnation. If we are committed to a program of discipleship—but the end is not the incarnational person and teachings of Jesus Christ as found in Scripture but rather our collective secular imagination—then our discipleship programs are meaningless. If we collaborate but only for the purpose of a sustainable business model and not about the business of modeling Christ's fullness of both grace and truth, then our collaboration is merely a financial expedient and lacks fidelity to the teleological purposes for which the Christian institution was established.

There comes a point when a church or denomination crosses the line and ceases to be Christian. Bonhoeffer, in *The Cost of Discipleship*, writes about his own denomination in Germany during the rise of the Third Reich when he contends, "We confess, that although our Church is orthodox as far as her doctrine of grace is concerned, we are no longer sure that we are members of a Church that follows Jesus its Lord" (p. 60).

Likewise, there comes a point where a school crosses the line from being Christian to becoming formerly Christian as has been detailed at length in works such as James Tunstead Burtchaell's *The Dying of the Light: The Disengagement of Colleges and Universities from Their Christian Churches* (1998). At some point an institution cannot continue to cede ground to the secular "headwinds" mentioned by Ream and Pattengale without becoming secular in everything but the marketing. Universities following any number of political and social currents are not communicating a biblical worldview. At that point they cease, in a very real way, to be Christian.

As we deliberate on the elements of this book that will perhaps help save the Christian college, seeking ways to Aspire, Imagine, Collaborate, and Illuminate, we need to remember that an institution can succeed in continuing operationally while ceasing to be Christian. And when it has ceased to be Christian in doctrine and deed, by default it cannot be saved, because it is already lost.

The title *The Anxious Middle* is reminiscent of the premise Jacques Ellul offers in *The Presence of the Kingdom*. Writing not many years after Bonhoeffer, Ellul also lived through the atrocities of the Nazi regime under the puppet government of Vichy France. Ellul writes that for the Christian, every circumstance is to be judged in the light of Christ's second coming. The parousia is more important than politics. According to Ellul, the Christian life does not spring from a "cause" but moves toward an "end" (p. 40). The whole of the Christian life "has only one aim, to be preserved unto the coming of the Lord Jesus Christ" (p. 43). Like Pattengale and Ream, when discussing the transformational engagement purpose of L'Abri, and the original Benedictine communities, Ellul states that a Christian's unique presence in the world becomes God's primary medium of action but only if the end is Christ.

The Anxious Middle is a practical playbook for boards and cabinets to use as they discuss how to address the moral questions facing their institutions. I would be so bold as to suggest that the preeminent moral question facing Christian colleges and universities today in America is how to stay fully engaged in an unapologetically Christ-centered mission, while at the same time remaining fully equal to the task of engaging the world. Doing so will demand we deliberate on Aspiration, Imagination, Collaboration, and Illumination while not losing our focus on the context in which they are all to be implemented—Incarnation.

Postscript 2

Linda A. Livingstone
Baylor University President

odd C. Ream and Jerry Pattengale identified a significant deficit in Christian higher education—a central, robust vision of discipleship that grounds and animates Christian universities. And they have offered fresh ideas on how to infuse this vision of discipleship into everything from student programming to marketing and campus communications. I found especially keen their insight that the size of the stories that animate a Christian college reveals the breadth of its witness in the lives of those it serves (p. 33).

I want to underscore three ideas from the book that resonated deeply with me—communal ownership, civil discourse, and unity in a diverse community.

In the second half of chapter 1, the authors explore *The Rule of St. Benedict* and its impact on Christian monastic communities. The authors note a "novelty" of the Rule: "Every monk is considered responsible for the entire community."

The crux of St. Benedict's proposition is that every member of the community is considered responsible for the *vision* and *mission* of the community. As a university president, I have a duty to articulate my campus' vision, embody it, and create engagement around it. But in a community of Christian faith, members collectively share responsibility for the mission and vision.

Let us apply this to discipleship on our campuses. At Christian colleges and universities, no single person is responsible for cultivating the moral imagination of the campus. Nor does the task of catechizing the student body rest squarely on the shoulders of the campus minister. Every member of the university bears responsibility in the discipleship process.

This framing of communal ownership has several benefits. First, it relieves pressure from our campus ministers, religion departments, spiritual life offices, and others who work in spiritual formation and pastoral care.

At Baylor, about fifteen students from our George W. Truett Theological Seminary sign up annually to live in our residence halls as chaplains. Each academic year, these chaplains live alongside our students. They are front-line responders during mental health struggles and unexpected deaths. They offer listening ears, counsel, and prayer for dozens and even hundreds of students in their residence halls. It can be a tremendous responsibility for these chaplains to bear, most of whom are in their twenties!

These chaplains are a vital component of the discipleship process. But they are one touchpoint in a long line of touchpoints extending from the time our students move into their dorms to their commencement ceremony. They join faculty members, staff members, local pastors, and others in a great cloud of witnesses in the lives of our students.

A second benefit to communal ownership is that it calls employees and students into *participation* in the lives and discipleship of their peers. An abiding culture of communal ownership reinforces the call to love our neighbors and to bear one another's burdens. And it affirms that everyone—from the registrar's office to research assistants and human resources professionals—has a role to play in discipleship.

A culture of communal ownership does not arise without concerted effort. For campus leaders, this means telling and retelling the story of the gospel, both at an institutional level and through the work of individual departments. And, of course, it means asking the Holy Spirit to spur on those we lead to take responsibility for the spiritual health of our campuses.

The second idea that resonated deeply with me is from the end of chapter 1: "The greater the sense of appreciation an institution has for its understanding of discipleship, the greater its eagerness to serve as a venue for such expression of discussion and debate. In essence, an understanding of discipleship fosters the hope needed to view such experiences as opportunities, not threats" (pp. 53–54).

This is a marvelous approach to discussing challenging ideas. A college campus is a marketplace of ideas, a unique locale to engage in vibrant, nuanced discussion. Vibrant, nuanced discussion requires a willingness to listen to the ideas of others. And active listening requires charity and compassion, Christian virtues our campuses actively seek to cultivate.

Christian higher education should be a national leader in civil discourse. The Christian college is an ideal venue for modeling thoughtful discourse in pursuit of God's truth.

On our campuses, our students are learning to take ownership for their beliefs. Many are evaluating their convictions seriously for the first time in their lives. They are living in a community of peers undergoing a similar process of moral formation. And they are surrounded by Christian scholars who have wrestled with the same hot-button topics.

A Christian institution of higher learning is the perfect forum to ask these questions. We are well-positioned to exhort students to exercise their God-given intellects in pursuit of God's truth. And we can train students to subject their ideas to the scrutiny of Christian community and the witness of Christian tradition.

Students are much more likely to arrive at sound, biblical conclusions if they sleuth out challenging questions with Christ-following scholars and a community of peers than if their moral formation occurs alone, without guidance on the internet.

Christian universities are also well-positioned to train faculty to discuss ideas rigorously and charitably. If our faculty can fathom all mysteries and all knowledge but do not show love in their discourse, the apostle Paul says they have gained nothing.

It is a deficit of discipleship if we do not train our campus community to confront challenging issues from a biblical, well-reasoned perspective. It is critical that we train them to think and give account for their convictions in a way that represents Christ. In doing so, we demonstrate our identity as Christians—"while we are a Kingdom First people, we are not a Kingdom Only people" (p. 62).

The final point I want to stress is one that the authors make multiple times: in cultivating the imagination of different sectors of a Christian university, "uniformity is never the goal" (p. 65).

Discipleship in student life offices looks different than discipleship in basketball gyms. Inviting philosophy professors to integrate faith into their teaching looks different than inviting computer science professors to integrate faith into their research. For campus discipleship to be effective, it must be contextualized.

Discipleship will also look different among professors of different Christian traditions. At Baylor, I celebrate the ecumenical nature of our faculty and staff. While we are firmly rooted in our Baptist history and tradition, we have a mosaic of Catholic, Methodist, Presbyterian, Baptist, Episcopal, Pentecostal, nondenominational, Anabaptist, and other Christian scholars at Baylor.

As Baylor's president, I want our faculty to feel empowered to model Baylor's Christian mission in ways that are authentic to their personal faith. Our campus' spiritual health does not require uniformity in expression. Rather, "the health of a Christian college is measured in larger part by a spirit of unity" (p. 85).

At Baylor, this looks like uniting faculty under a common vision: to educate men and women for worldwide leadership and service by integrating academic excellence and Christian commitment within a caring community. Unity of vision and purpose allows for each member of our body to perform a diversity of functions while anchored in the enduring truth of God's Word.

These were just three of the dozens of points made throughout *The Anxious Middle* that resonated with and challenged me. Thank you to Todd, Jerry, and everyone else involved in producing this terrific book.

Postscript 3

Beck A. Taylor
Samford University President

I n my thirteen years as a university president, I have had the opportunity to lead two prominent Christ-centered institutions through comprehensive strategic planning exercises. In each case, our efforts were centered upon sustaining and advancing the unique, transformative ways such places can impact the lives of students and other constituencies for the cause of Christ.

My experience confirms that such planning efforts are, at their best, organic, generative, and healthy as organizations dream about the future and consider ways to allocate scarce resources to advance institutional priorities. Strategy sessions with various and diverse stakeholders can also be susceptible to fear, confusion, protectionism, and the inability to see beyond current limitations. Effective strategic planning simultaneously acknowledges the specific contexts that institutions face, including real constraints and hopeful opportunities, striking a balance between debilitating deficit thinking and misplaced toxic enthusiasm. It is hard to imagine any institution that seeks excellence in higher education reaching its aspirational goals without considerable time and energy devoted to planning for its future.

"Unless the Lord builds the house," the psalmist reminds us, "the builders labor in vain" (Ps 127:1, NIV). Strategic planning efforts at Christ-centered colleges and universities can and should follow well-tested methodologies and seek to employ effective tools to create roadmaps for the future. Unless our kinds of institutions also make concerted efforts to rely heavily upon prayer, spiritual inspiration, and theological discernment, we simultaneously fail to use all of the resources available to faithful people and institutions and miss an opportunity to find meaningful worship and effective witness to the Lord of all creation and the ultimate author of our institutional narratives.

The authors of this volume, drawing upon Dietrich Bonhoeffer's inspired sermons on Genesis, provide a useful and refreshing scaffolding or schema upon which to host strategic questions and conversations regarding the future of Christian higher education and the intellectual and spiritual resources that will serve Christian colleges and universities well as they embark on strategy formation and implementation. Avoiding the temptation to dive straight into important topics like teaching excellence, faith-learning integration, sustainable financial models, and cultural engagement, Todd Ream and Jerry Pattengale encourage us to start our campus conversations with more basic and fundamental questions of meaning and purpose, questions that should be at the heart of any faithful institution. By encouraging us to center our initial planning conversations around the topics of aspiration, imagination, collaboration, and illumination, Ream and Pattengale remind us to focus first on those animating characteristics that should truly differentiate institutions that profess the lordship of Jesus Christ. In this postscript, I offer a few brief thoughts under each of the four headings based upon my own observations and experiences.

Aspiration

Of the four areas Ream and Pattengale draw our attention to, it is perhaps the exercise of aspiration that may cause institutions devoted to academic excellence, freedom of inquiry, and civil disagreement the most trouble. If the primary role of Christ-centered higher education is to engage in spiritual formation and discipleship, how are those priorities squared and reconciled with constituencies on campus that are also worried that such efforts will dilute the academic mission or reputation of a college or university? Merely stating that a university has a bent toward evangelism, or more explicitly that all students should be exposed to the gospel of Christ, could raise alarms at faithful institutions that are also well known for academic pursuits. An institution's founding *by* the church and *for* the church does not compel it to *be* a church, or so the argument goes.

Despite these challenges and like Ream and Pattengale, I contend that those colleges and universities for whom the lordship of Christ is the central animating feature of their mission and identity should, in fact, claim Christian discipleship—in all its forms and in the broadest sense—as the primary goal. Like Bonhoeffer, and as supported by Ream and Pattengale, although the outputs of the academy that would include quality instruction, research discovery, and applied learning are valuable outcomes and should be included in the array of institutional activities that are celebrated, if the Christian college or university does not also focus its energies in helping students discern "clear conceptions of what it means for God to be God, for humans to be God's creation, and for humans to share in right relations with God," then the Christian academy cannot stand distinctly from the secular one, and, by extension, there is no compelling feature that would warrant the time, energy, and other resources to further differentiate a Christian institution from its worldly peers.

Imagination

If expressing Christian institutions' shared aspiration to prioritize the spiritual formation of their students is the tallest task of the four areas outlined in this book, then perhaps it is also true that finding expression for the creative imaginations of the very same institutions is the activity that brings the most unity, excitement, and energy in the planning process. In my experience, convening conversations across multiple stakeholder groups that attempt to brainstorm and prioritize creative expressions for the academic enterprise is not a difficult task. Students, employees, alumni, and community members are never short of ideas about how the university can do new things or improve existing efforts. Thinking imaginatively about how to improve access to study-away opportunities, increase participation in leadership training, or improve employee satisfaction comes easily to most academics and others who are engaged and invested in their institution's success. Finding enough resources to fund all of the ideas is much harder, and often difficult choices must be made. As our authors remind us, these generative conversations full of "hopeful imagination" must be grounded in the institution's responsibility to encourage discipleship, and once this foundation is properly laid, then creative and inspiring efforts to contribute to truth, goodness, and beauty can follow.

Although resource constraints are real and strategic tradeoffs abound, the most significant challenge I have perceived among Christian colleges and universities when articulating their plans is the inability to think big enough. Deficit mindsets are pervasive in nonprofit settings. Conversations that center on setting transformative goals often reduce to managing budget constraints rather than thinking about growth, opportunity, and impact. This is a spiritual limitation as much as it is a practical one. Those of us who work at Christ-centered colleges and universities will be quick to express our confidence in the transformative work that happens daily on our campuses—lives are changed, communities are strengthened, and the kingdom of God is more fully realized. We would also quickly give credit for these wonderful outcomes to the Lord. But too often, when it comes to imagining an even greater impact, an enlarged and even outsize role in the higher education arena, conservatism, fear, and negativism can stifle otherwise exciting, impactful, and achievable visions. Particularly at a time when the survival of our institutions is in question, leaders must be imagining and acting to realize bold and ambitious visions for their institutions.

Collaboration

Higher education is inherently cooperative. The sharing of teaching and research findings with colleagues and institutions is commonplace. Many discipline-specific associations encourage such collaboration with conferences and workshops. Institutional associations like the Council for Christian Colleges and Universities and Council of Independent Colleges also work with member institutions to share information. Colleges and universities frequently publish their institutional strategic plans, including working details, on websites for outsiders to digest. Most accrediting bodies encourage the sharing of best practices, even among schools that compete with one another for students. There is no doubt that institutions can get "locked into institutional structures and cultures," as Ream and Pattengale suggest, but at least our collective DNA orients us toward a more collaborative posture.

Perhaps the area of collaboration that represents the greatest opportunity for mission alignment for the Christian university, but also represents the area where many faithful institutions are giving little effort, is cooperation with the local church. Most if not all Christian colleges and universities were established to do just that—to support the sponsoring denomination and local churches in the training of clergy, to provide for general education that would equip congregations to contribute to the common good, and to support and encourage a moral climate that embodied Christian teaching.

Perhaps because of the tensions I mentioned previously concerning the overt naming of Christian discipleship as a strategic priority, institutions may have over time distanced themselves from the life and mission of the local church. The Lilly Endowment is one of several organizations that gives significant funding to colleges and universities that support engagement with ordained and lay leaders, congregations, and ministerial associations.

Collaboration with local churches can provide connections and relationships that can enrich many of the missional elements already highlighted in this volume.

Illumination

Matthew 5:15 (NIV) records Jesus saying, "Neither do people light a lamp and put it under a bowl. Instead they put it on its stand, and it gives light to everyone in the house." Proclamation has always been a central activity of the Christian life. As we have discussed, Christ-centered colleges and universities must commit to sharing the gospel, but that is not the only good news we have to share. The stories of transformation, blessing, community engagement, and impact can serve as a witness to our faith while also encouraging stakeholders to remain engaged and inspired.

In my experience, Christian institutions can confuse humility with ineffective communication and marketing. Is it unseemly to share the accomplishments of faculty and students to a world that often questions the relevance of the Christian academy? We have great stories to tell, and our ability to communicate the wonderful and inspiring things happening on our campuses can encourage others to give generously and to support public policy critical to our survival, and lead to more institutional aspiration, imagination, and collaboration. Christian colleges and universities are well served as they invest in compelling marketing and communications plans.

Final Thought

Ream and Pattengale urge us to live faithfully in the "anxious middle." In Philippians 4:6–7 (NIV), Paul exhorts us: "Do not be anxious about anything, but in everything, by prayer and petition, with thanksgiving, present your requests to God. And the peace of God, which transcends all understanding, will guard your hearts and your minds in Christ Jesus." Let the cause of Christian higher education serve as the much-needed remedy for the world's anxiety.

Notes

Foreword

1 Dietrich Bonhoeffer, "Protestantism without Reformation," in *No Rusty Swords: Letters, Lectures, and Notes, 1928–1936*, ed. Edwin H. Robertson (New York: Harper & Row, 1965), 117–18.

Introduction

1 George M. Marsden, "How to Save the Christian College—Request for Input," email response to authors, 2022.

2 The journal also added a robust web presence in 2020, reaching thousands more readers monthly. Currently some thirteen thousand individuals receive the "Christ Animated Learning" posts Monday through Friday with an average daily click-through rate of thirty-five hundred individuals.

3 In this book, we will employ the phrase "the Christian college" as representative of all institutions that reference themselves as Christian colleges and universities. When using that phrase, we are referencing all institutions regardless of their Christian tradition, organizational structure, and geographic location. Such a phrase is employed for the sake of consistency and convenience as well as offering a historic acknowledgment of the movement's origins.

4   Christian College Consortium, "Welcome to the Christian College Consortium," https://www.ccconsortium.org.

5   For more details, see James A. Patterson, *Shining Lights: A History of the Council for Christian Colleges and Universities* (Grand Rapids: Baker Academic, 2001); and William Ringenberg, *The Christian College: A History of Protestant Higher Education in America* (Grand Rapids: Baker Academic, 2006).

6   Council for Christian Colleges and Universities, "Our Work and Mission," https://www.cccu.org/about.

7   "Why Christian Colleges Are Booming: Parents Want a Safe Haven but These Schools Have a Higher Purpose," *Christianity Today*, April 26, 1999, https://www.christianitytoday.com/ct/1999/april26/9t5026.html.

8   "Why Christian Colleges Are Booming."

9   Lindsay Ellis, "How the Great Recession Reshaped American Higher Education," *Chronicle of Higher Education*, September 14, 2018, https://www.chronicle.com/article/how-the-great-recession-reshaped-american-higher-education/. This reality was all too familiar with financial markets' sharp downturn in the summer of 2022 and the implosion of cryptocurrency as this book was being drafted.

10 See works such as Nathan D. Grawe, *Demographics and the Demand for Higher Education* (Baltimore: Johns Hopkins University Press, 2018); and Robert Zemsky, Susan Shaman, and Susan Campbell Baldridge, *The College Stress Test: Tracking Institutional Futures across a Crowded Market* (Baltimore: Johns Hopkins University Press, 2020).

11 National Association of College and University Business Officers, "2021 Tuition Discounting Study," https://www.nacubo.org/Research/2021/NACUBO%20Tuition%20Discounting%20Study.

12 With the U.S. Supreme Court's *Dobbs v. Jackson* (2022) decision, the significance of this concern is likely in great flux and, with the other concerns noted, merits close observation.

13 John Garvey and Philip Ryken, "An Evangelical-Catholic Stand on Liberty," *Wall Street Journal*, July 19, 2012, https://www.wsj.com/articles/SB10001424052702303933704577533251292715324.

14 Shaila Dewan, "United Church of Christ Backs Same-Sex Marriage," *New York Times*, July 5, 2005, https://www.nytimes.com/2005/07/05/us/united-church-of-christ-backs-samesex-marriage.html.

15 David Dawson, "Episcopalians Set to Be First Big U.S. Church to Bless Gay Marriage," *Reuters*, July 9, 2012, https://www.reuters.com/article/usa-religion-gaymarriage/episcopalians-set-to-be-first-big-u-s-church-to-bless-gay-marriage-idINDEE86901020120710.

16 Timothy Larsen, "The Evangelical Reception of Dietrich Bonhoeffer," in *Bonhoeffer, Christ, and Culture*, ed. Keith L. Johnson and Timothy Larsen (Downers Grove, Ill.: InterVarsity, 2013), 46–47. See also Stephen R. Haynes, *The Bonhoeffer Phenomenon: Portraits of a Saint* (Minneapolis: Fortress, 2004); and *The Battle for Bonhoeffer: Debating Discipleship in the Age of Trump* (Grand Rapids: Eerdmans, 2018).

17 For more details, see Karl Barth, *The Epistle to the Romans* (New York: Oxford University Press, 1968). Originally published in German in 1919, Barth's theological exegesis of Romans was his initial attempt to break with Protestant liberalism and the historical-critical studies of Scripture that date back at least to 1835 and the publication of D. F. Strauss, *The Life of Jesus, Critically Examined*. For further evidence of Bonhoeffer's affinity for Barth's approach, see Dietrich Bonhoeffer, "Letter to Karl Barth, December 24, 1932," in *Berlin: 1932–1933* (Minneapolis: Fortress, 2009), 81–82.

18 John W. de Gruchy, "Editor's Introduction," in Dietrich Bonhoeffer, *Creation and Fall* (Minneapolis: Fortress, 2004), 8.

19 de Gruchy, "Editor's Introduction," in Bonhoeffer, *Creation and Fall*, 9. See also Eberhard Bethge, *Dietrich Bonhoeffer: A Biography* (Minneapolis: Fortress, 2000); and Charles Marsh, *Strange Glory: A Life of Dietrich Bonhoeffer* (New York: Alfred A. Knopf, 2014).

20 William L. Shirer, *The Rise and Fall of the Third Reich: A History of Nazi Germany* (New York: Simon & Schuster, 2011), 187.

21 The literature concerning strategic planning as found in business and education proves essential to consider when preparing for such processes. For example, the Society for

College and University Planning has a large number of valuable resources available for download under the "Learning Resources" tab on their website, www.scup.org. Such processes on Christian college and university campuses, however, also need to be theologically informed for the missions of those institutions to be exercised to their fullest this side of eternity. In essence, such institutions otherwise run the risk of dropping the horizon of possibility too low. To this end, Jürgen Moltmann wrote, hope and planning "live with each other and for each other. Without specific goals toward which hope is directed, there can be no decision about the possibilities of planning; but without planning, there can be no realistic hope." The presence, definition, and role the virtue of hope plays in the planning process thus becomes critical. For more details, see Moltmann, *Hope and Planning* (New York: Harper & Row, 1971), 178.

22 Wendy Fischman and Howard Gardner, *The Real World of College: What Higher Education Is and What It Can Be* (Cambridge, Mass.: MIT Press, 2022), xi.

23 Fischman and Gardner, *Real World of College*, xvi.

24 Fischman and Gardner, *Real World of College*, xvi.

25 Richard J. Light and Allison Jegla, *Becoming Great Universities: Small Steps for Sustained Excellence* (Princeton, N.J.: Princeton University Press, 2022), 3.

26 Bonhoeffer, *Creation and Fall*, 29.

27 Bonhoeffer, *Creation and Fall*, 58.

28 Bonhoeffer, *Creation and Fall*, 97.

29 Bonhoeffer, *Creation and Fall*, 97.

30 Bonhoeffer, *Creation and Fall*, 145.

1 Aspiration

1 Dietrich Bonhoeffer, "Sermon on Judges 6:15–16; 7:2; 8:23," in *Berlin*, 448.

2 Bonhoeffer, "Sermon on Judges," 449.

3 Bonhoeffer, "Sermon on Judges," 450.

4 Bonhoeffer, "Sermon on Judges," 449.

5 Bonhoeffer, "Sermon on Judges," 449.

6   We will refrain from naming particular institutions and plans at this point perhaps for no greater reason than politeness or perhaps sentimentality. Although we are supportive of terms and phrases such as *entrepreneurial playing* and *increasing access*, for example, playing prominent roles in such plans, we are first addressing underlying questions: To what end does a Christian college strive to be entrepreneurial and/or increase access? In essence, are aspirations to be entrepreneurial and/or increase access given life and meaning by a larger understanding of discipleship? Or are they captive to the economic and/or political interests?

7   Bonhoeffer, "Sermon on Judges," 449.

8   Bonhoeffer, *Creation and Fall*, 21.

9   Bonhoeffer, *Creation and Fall*, 22.

10   Bonhoeffer, *Creation and Fall*, 22.

11   Bonhoeffer, *Creation and Fall*, 22.

12   Bonhoeffer, *Creation and Fall*, 22.

13   Bonhoeffer, *Creation and Fall*, 22.

14   Bonhoeffer, *Creation and Fall*, 30.

15   Bonhoeffer, *Creation and Fall*, 29 (italics original).

16   Bonhoeffer, *Creation and Fall*, 33 (italics original).

17   Bonhoeffer, *Creation and Fall*, 32.

18   Bonhoeffer, *Creation and Fall*, 33 and 34.

19   Bonhoeffer, *Creation and Fall*, 35.

20   Bonhoeffer, *Creation and Fall*.

21   Bonhoeffer, *Creation and Fall*, 36.

22   Bonhoeffer, *Creation and Fall*, 39. The term *being* as used by Bonhoeffer in this sense is reflective of Martin Heidegger's concept of *being* as detailed in *Being and Time*. Originally published in 1927, Heidegger's *Being and Time* was his effort to grapple with what he believed was philosophy's most fundamental question—what does it mean to exist? His work then led to a resurgence of the subdiscipline in philosophy of ontology.

23   Bonhoeffer, *Creation and Fall*, 39.

24   Bonhoeffer, *Creation and Fall*, 39.

25   Many modern examples could be given. Two here suffice, both from the northwest. Multnomah University (MU) in Portland,

Oregon, is fighting for its survival. Jerry Pattengale and Alan Hotchkiss met with MU's new president, Eric Joseph, and discussed this reality on April 20, 2022. Alan is president of the large and effective Africa New Life Ministry (Rwanda) and is MU's Alumnus of the Year (2020). While Dr. Joseph ("EJ") remains hopeful and expectant for MU's future, the region's accrediting bodies and educational outlets have hampered the school's capacity for recruiting students—mainly resulting from the closure of MU's education and music programs. This is the same school widely known for its graduates launching the Jesus Project and Africa New Life (Pastor Charles Buregeya Mugisha, MU alumnus), launching the Multnomah Press, and having a major involvement in the Luis Palau organization. A similar scenario has taken place at Trinity Western University (TWU) near Vancouver, British Columbia. Through a case that played out in international media, TWU's law school was challenged through the Canadian Supreme Court due to its faith component. Though initially winning, eventually it lost its bid to open a Christian law school. See Kate Shellnutt, "Canada's Supreme Court Rejects Country's Only Christian Law School," *Christianity Today*, June 15, 2018. However, TWU maintains ten institutes or centers that continue their impact in addressing various needs. (See https://www.twu.ca/research/institutes-and -centres.) For example, the Dead Sea Scrolls Centre has a longstanding history of involving top scholars and engagement in important literature. Likewise, the Institute of Indigenous Issues and Perspectives (Canada/Australia/New Zealand) maintains an important presence in helping the Aboriginal, First Nations, Inuit, Metis, Māori, and Torres Strait Islander populations.

26 A useful summary with links, resources, and analysis is found at George Cyprian Alston, "Rule of St. Benedict," in *The Catholic Encyclopedia*, vol. 2 (New York: Robert Appleton Company, 1907), http://www.newadvent.org/cathen/02436a.htm. For a simple list of the contents of the seventy-three chapters, see "Analysis of the Rule."

27 Rod Dreher, *The Benedict Option: A Strategy for Christians in a Post-Christian Nation* (New York: Sentinel, 2017). A response to Dreher's argument is found in Patrick Henry, *Benedictine*

Options: Learning to Live from the Sons and Daughters of Saints Benedict and Scholastica (Collegeville, Minn.: Liturgical, 2021).

28 The dates of his death vary, such as ca. 560 in S. Zincone, "Benedict of Nursia," in *Encyclopedia of Ancient Christianity*, vol. 1, ed. Angelo Di Berardino (Downers Grove, Ill.: IVP Academic, 2014), 352–53.

29 For a helpful list of primary sources for Benedict of Nursia, see I. G. Smith, "Benedictus of Nursia: Abbott [*sic*] of Monte Cassino," in *A Dictionary of Early Christian Biography and Literature to the End of the Sixth Century A.D., with an Account of the Principal Sects and Heresies*, ed. Henry Wace and William C. Piercy (originally *A Dictionary of Christian Biography and Literature* [London: John Murray, 1911; repr., Peabody, Mass.: Hendrickson, 1999, 130–32]).

30 Dreher, *Benedict Option*, 19. See Emma Green's candid review of Dreher's "radical critique of American culture" (and his lamenting of the sexual revolution) in "The Christian Retreat from Public Life," *Atlantic*, February 22, 2017, https://www .theatlantic.com/politics/archive/2017/02/benedict-option/ 517290/. She concludes, "Many people, including some Christians, feel that knowing, befriending, playing with, and learning alongside people who are different from them adds to their faith, not that it threatens it. For all their power and appeal, Dreher's monastery walls may be too high, and his mountain pass too narrow."

31 Diarmaid MacCulloch, *Christianity: The First Three Thousand Years* (New York: Penguin: 2009), 317.

32 Justo L. Gonzalez, *The Story of Christianity*, vol. 1, *The Early Church to the Dawn of the Reformation* (New York: HarperOne, 2010), 278.

33 Zincone, "Benedict of Nursia," in Di Berardino, *Encyclopedia*, 352.

34 These have been renamed, but the original names still seem to be the common reference points.

35 These are massive. Both the Catholic and Lutheran breviaries are four volumes (which prompted a one-volume traveling version for the monks in the Middle Ages).

36 MacCulloch, *Christianity*, 318.

37 MacCulloch, *Christianity*, 295. See also 1082, n. 15.

38 Kate Shellnutt, "Eat, Pray, Code: Rule of St. Benedict Becomes Tech Developer's Community Guidelines," *Christianity Today*, October 26, 2020, https://www.christianitytoday.com/news/2018/october/sqlite-benedict-rule-code-ethics-hipp-developer-christian.html.

39 Shellnutt, "Eat, Pray." A simple list of the seventy-three rules (or "tools") are given.

40 Edith Schaeffer has well documented the history and impact of L'Abri in her books: *L'Abri* (Wheaton, Ill.: Tyndale, 1969; expanded ed., Westchester, Ill.: Crossway, 1992); *The Tapestry* (Waco, Tex.: Word, 1981). Also see their son's reflections in Frank Schaeffer, *Crazy for God* (Cambridge, Mass.: Perseus, 2007). Also see Schaeffer's novel, *Portofino* (New York: Berkeley, 1996); and Scott Burson's interaction with it in *All about the Bass: Searching for Treble in the Midst of a Pounding Culture War* (Eugene, Ore.: Cascade, 2021), 59–61. Ultimately, the theological differences in responding to these cultural challenges prompt Burson to reintroduce Francis Schaeffer's "Final Apologetic" of "Christian unity and love that flows between fellow believers." Besides the numerous works and tapes by Francis Schaeffer, see Scott R. Burson and Jerry L. Walls, *C. S. Lewis and Francis Schaeffer: Lessons for a New Century from the Most Influential Apologists of Our Time* (Downers Grove, Ill.: InterVarsity, 1998). Barry Hankins also authored an impressive biography of Schaeffer, *Francis Schaeffer and the Shaping of Evangelical America* (Grand Rapids: Eerdmans, 2008).

41 Miroslav Volf, *A Public Faith: How Followers of Christ Should Serve the Common Good* (Grand Rapids: Brazos, 2011), 65. For a discussion of Kronman's book and thesis, see Jerry Pattengale, "The Big Questions: Have Our Colleges and Universities Lost Sight of Their Purpose?" *Books and Culture*, November–December, 2009, a review of Anthony Kronman's *Education's End: Why Our Colleges and Universities Have Given Up on the Meaning of Life* (New Haven, Conn.: Yale University Press, 2008).

42 Eric Cunningham, quoted in Perry L. Glanzer and Nathan F. Alleman, *The Outrageous Idea of Christian Teaching* (New York: Oxford University Press, 2019), 63.

43 Andy Crouch, *Culture Making: Recovering Our Creative Calling* (Downers Grove, Ill.: InterVarsity, 2008), 86.

44 Crouch, *Culture Making*, 87.

45 Steven Garber, *The Fabric of Faithfulness: Weaving Together Belief and Behavior during the University Years* (Downers Grove, Ill.: InterVarsity, 1996), 30–31.

46 Russ Pulliam, "A Voice in the Wilderness," *Indianapolis Star*, May 23, 1984. Pulliam is a lifelong journalist and oversees his family's Pulliam Journalism Fellowship. He lived at L'Abri in the British Isles from March to April 1977. For the purpose of our current discussion, his reflection on Schaeffer's impact points us to the new message (really, as old as the world) that "God is over all of life" and that the Bible intersects directly with social issues. In "Francis Schaeffer's Influence on My Life," he points to two of Schaeffer's twenty-two books that proved riveting in this personal quest (and among students nationally) for a deeper meaning: *The God Who Is There* and *Escape from Reason*. See Pulliam, "Francis Schaeffer's Influence on My Life," *Covenanter Witness*, April 1984, 1.

47 L'Abri Fellowship International, at https://www.labri.org/.

48 Hankins, *Francis Schaeffer*, x.

49 Dreher, *Benedict Option*, 168.

50 The Consortium of Christian Study Centers was founded in 1994, and 85 percent of the centers attended its 2021 conference; see https://cscmovement.org/who-we-are/.

51 Consortium of Christian Study Centers, https://cscmovement .org/who-we-are/.

52 David C. Mahan, "University Ministry and the Evangelical Mind" (with the second section by Donald Smedley), in *The State of the Evangelical Mind: Reflections on the Past, Prospects for the Future*, ed. Todd C. Ream, Jerry Pattengale, and Christopher J. Devers (Downers Grove, Ill.: InterVarsity, 2018), 70.

53 Consortium of Christian Study Centers, https://cscmovement .org/who-we-are/.

54 2 Cor 10:5 (RSV).

55 For more nuanced accounts of this concern than space here can afford, please see the afterword in Mark A. Noll, *The Scandal of*

the Evangelical Mind, rev. ed. (Grand Rapids: Eerdmans, 2022); and the epilogue in George A. Marsden, *The Soul of the American University Revisited: From Protestant to Postsecular* (New York: Oxford University Press, 2021).

56 In *The Second Mountain: The Quest for a Moral Life* (New York: Random House, 2019), David Brooks addresses this plague facing the Christian college; see esp. 256–57.

57 Credit for this line goes to Sam Waterston's character, Charlie Skinner, in season 1, episode 10 ("The Greater Fool") of *The Newsroom*.

58 In *Higher Education in America* (Princeton, N.J.: Princeton University Press, 2013), Derek Bok reviews all of the extant data concerning the impact the practice of research has on the practice of teaching. The common wisdom he explores is whether a commitment to research leads to a decrease in commitment to teaching. Bok found no such decrease existed. If anything, he found a commitment to research refreshes teaching and improves its quality.

2 Imagination

1 Dietrich Bonhoeffer, "Letter to Reinhold Niebuhr, February 6, 1933," in *Berlin*, 94–95.

2 Dietrich Bonhoeffer, "Letter to Erwin Sutz, April 14, 1933," in *Berlin*, 101.

3 By imagination, we are not referring to a daydreaming exercise of wishful thinking. In contrast, drawing from a definition proposed by Charles Taylor in *Modern Social Imaginaries* (Durham, N.C.: Duke University Press, 2004), we are referring to "the ways people imagine their social existence, how they fit together with others, how things go on between them and their fellows, the expectations that are normally met, and the deeper normative notions and images which underlie these expectations" (23). In addition, we are grateful for the ways that James K. A. Smith and Daniel S. Hendrickson, S.J., unpacked the ramifications of Taylor's thinking concerning the imagination in their respective books, *Desiring the Kingdom: Worship, Worldview, and Cultural Formation* (Grand Rapids: Baker Academic, 2009); and *Jesuit*

Higher Education in a Secular Age: A Response to Charles Taylor and the Crisis of Fullness (Washington, D.C.: Georgetown University Press, 2022). This chapter will build toward that understanding of the imagination as elucidated by Taylor, Smith, and Hendrickson.

4   Bonhoeffer, "Sermon on Judges," 448.
5   Bonhoeffer, "Sermon on Judges," 464.
6   Bonhoeffer, "Sermon on Judges," 464.
7   Bonhoeffer, "Sermon on Judges," 464.
8   Bonhoeffer, "Sermon on Judges," 464.
9   Bonhoeffer, "Sermon on Judges," 465.
10 Bonhoeffer, "Sermon on Judges," 465.
11 Bonhoeffer, "Sermon on Judges," 465.
12 Bonhoeffer, "Sermon on Judges," 465.
13 Bonhoeffer, "Sermon on Judges," 465.
14 Bonhoeffer, "Sermon on Judges," 465.
15 John I. Jenkins, C.S.C., "Inaugural Address of Rev. John I. Jenkins, C.S.C.," University of Notre Dame, Office of the President, https://president.nd.edu/homilies-writings-addresses/inaugural-address-of-rev-john-i-jenkins-c-s-c/.
16 Bonhoeffer, *Creation and Fall*, 61.
17 Bonhoeffer, *Creation and Fall*, 62.
18 Bonhoeffer, *Creation and Fall*, 63.
19 Although his work has great merit, here we would point to the work of Erich Przywara, S.J., as exemplified in his later 1962 book originally published in German, *Analogia Entis: Metaphysics; Original Structure and Universal Rhythm* (Grand Rapids: Eerdmans, 2014). Przywara also had a considerable impact on theologians such as Hans Urs von Balthasar.
20 Bonhoeffer, *Creation and Fall*, 65.
21 For example, on Thursday, June 23, 2022, the U.S. Supreme Court ruled in *New York State Rifle & Pistol Association v. Bruen* that the U.S. Constitution, via its Second Amendment, conferred upon citizens the right to carry handguns outside of their homes for self-defense. The next day, the court ruled in *Dobbs v. Jackson* that the Constitution, via its Fourteenth Amendment, did not confer upon citizens the right to an abortion. Beyond a

few philosophically consistent libertarians, gun rights advocates and abortion rights advocates may rarely find themselves to be fellow political travelers.

22 Bonhoeffer, *Creation and Fall*, 67.

23 Bonhoeffer, *Creation and Fall*, 67.

24 Hendrickson, *Jesuit Higher Education*, 165.

25 Martin Luther attended a school of the Brethren in Magdeburg (1478–1479). While Erasmus passed through the hostels of the Brethren, his various college experiences were certainly a major part of his development. D. D. Post, a key voice on the *Devotio Moderna* associated with the Brethren, warns of an overreach on the Common Life experience in his treatment of Wessel Gansfort (d. 1489). Though rather committed to the Brethren of the Common Life, Gansfort did spend twenty-five years at universities. He also claims of 1489: "In actual fact this marks the end of the history of the Brethren. They then lose their independent entity. In the last part of the fifteenth and the first quarter of the sixteenth centuries, the Brotherhood was absorbed into the intellectual and religious currents to which Humanism and the Reformation gave rise." D. D. Post, *Devotio Moderna: Confrontation with Reformation and Humanism* (Leiden: Brill, 1968), 25, 49. Nicholas of Cusa died in 1464, à Kempis in 1471, and Erasmus in 1536—thus any influence was in posthumous generations from Groote. See William M. Landeen, "Martin Luther's Intervention in [on] Behalf of the Brethren of the Common Life in Herford," *Andrews University Seminary Studies* 22, no. 1 (1984): 81–97, https://www.andrews.edu/library/car/cardigital/Periodicals/AUSS/1984-1/1984-1-10.pdf. Others make the case for the Brethren's influence on John Calvin. See Kenneth A. Strand, "John Calvin and the Brethren of the Common Life," Andrews University (pending publication), https://digitalcommons.andrews.edu/cgi/viewcontent.cgi?referer=&httpsredir=1&article=1309&context=auss.

26 Groote stipulated in his gifted estate's documents that he would commit only two rooms for his own use (sleep and administration of his activities) and that it would not be a new religious "order," which needed papal approval.

27 Harry Stout, email exchange with Jerry Pattengale, June 29–30, 2022.

28 Erasmus entered the Brethren community at age twenty-three. In England, he lived with Lord Chancellor Sir Thomas More, who encouraged him to write his opus, *In Praise of Folly.*

29 "Erasmus: Pious Humanist Who Sparked the Reformation," *Christianity Today,* https://www.christianitytoday.com/history/people/scholarsandscientists/erasmus.html.

30 "Erasmus: Pious Humanist."

31 For example, see "CCCU Forms Innovative Partnership with Ed Tech Company CampusEDU," CCCU, October 5, 2020, www.cccu.org/news-updates/cccu-forms-innovative-partnership-ed-tech-company-campusedu/; and www.campusedu.com.

32 Nikolaus Staubach, *The Reception of the Church Fathers in the West: From the Carolingians to the Maurists,* ed. Irena Dorota Backus, 2 vols. (Leiden: Brill, 1997), 1:406ff. Also see John H. Van Engen, *Devotio Moderna: Basic Writings,* Classics of Western Spirituality (New York: Paulist, 1988), 26.

33 See Glenn Martin, *Prevailing Worldviews* (Marion, Ind.: Triangle, 2006); and Jerry Pattengale, "The Capitol Offense: A Christian Professor's Warning 50 Years Ago," *Religion News Service,* January 27, 2021, https://religionnews.com/2021/01/27/the-capitol-offense-a-christian-professors-warning-50-years-ago/.

34 A sample is found in the binder fragments under the purview of the Museum of the Bible. This reflects the extremes of Scholasticism and is not intended to diminish the work of early Scholastics in the lineage of Aquinas, i.e., great thinkers such as Peter Lombard (c. 1100–1160), Bonaventure (c. 1217–1274), Albert Magnus (or "the Great" 1206–1280), John Duns Scotus (c. 1266–1308), and William of Ockham (d. 1347). See Stephen E. Lahey, "Thomas Aquinas: A Gallery of Scholastic Superstars," *Christian History* 78 (2002), https://christianhistoryinstitute.org/magazine/article/thomas-aquinas-gallery-of-scholastic-superstars. There are obviously varying views on Scholastics and their approach, and their impact on education is immense (not least being Abelard's *Sic et Non*). A host of Reformed scholars endorse the value of bringing the authority of Scriptures and

authoritative voices of the past to help with modern and future discussions. See Bobby Grow's post from an Evangelical Calvinist's perspective: "A Boring Post: Are Evangelical Calvinists More 'Scholastic' than the Scholastics Today?" *Athanasian Reformed*, February 14, 2013, https://growrag.wordpress.com/2013/02/14/a-boring-post-are-evangelical-calvinists-more-scholastic-than-the-scholastics-of-today/amp/.

35 Adapted from volume 1 of Jerry Pattengale, *A History of World Civilizations* (forthcoming).

36 See John Van Engen, *Sisters and Brothers of the Common Life: The Devotio Moderna and the World of the Later Middle Ages*, Middle Ages Series (Philadelphia: University of Pennsylvania Press, 2008). Also see the review by Susan Folkerts in *Journal of Religion* 91 (2011): 550–52. For a helpful literature review, see Willis Miller, *Devotio Moderna: The Cornerstone of the Reformation* (master's thesis, George Fox University, 2008), 1, 4–13 (note that he claims rather strong influence on Humanism and an inextricable link to the Reformation—claims much debated by various authors).

37 Van Engen, *Sisters and Brothers*, 307.

38 Miller, *Devotio Moderna*, 22.

39 Ruysbroeck's work at Groenendael is credited with the inspiration of the Devout Windesheim monasteries.

40 Gordon Leff et al., *The Medieval Church: Universities, Heresy, and the Religious Life; Essays in Honour of Gordon Leff*, Studies in Church History, Ecclesiastical History Society, Subsidia 11 (Woodbridge, U.K.: Boydell, 1999), 144.

41 See İ. Semih Akçomak, Dinand Webbink, and Bas ter Weel, "Why Did the Netherlands Develop So Early? The Legacy of the Brethren of the Common Life" (discussion paper, IZA, January 2013, https://docs.iza.org/dp7167.pdf); the authors claim, "Our empirical estimates provide evidence that the BCL has contributed to the uniquely and early high rates of literacy in the Low Countries in the decades before the amazing development of the Dutch Republic in the seventeenth century. In addition, we find positive effects of the BCL on early book production and on city growth in the fifteenth and sixteenth centuries. Finally,

we find that cities with BCL-roots significantly earlier joined the Dutch Revolt against the Habsburg Rulers" (p. i, in the abstract). (CGEH refers to Centre for Global Economic History.)

42 Katherine Schaeffer, "Ten Facts about Today's College Graduates," Pew Research Center, April 12, 2022, https://www.pewresearch.org/fact-tank/2022/04/12/10-facts-about-todays-college-graduates/. In 2021, the earning gap between individuals ages 22 to 27 with a bachelor's degree but no further education and those with only a high school diploma was $52,000 to $30,000.

43 See the various Church of the Highlands sites, including https://highlandscollege.com/highlands-college-graduates-over-400-trained-leaders-ready-for-ministry/.

44 Thirdmill has more than fifty full-time and part-time employees. It sprung from Janie Pillow's vision; Richard Pratt (president) and others have implemented it; see https://thirdmill.org/mission/.

45 CCCU homepage, https://www.cccu.org/about/#heading-our-work-and-mission-0.

46 Jerry Shepherd was regional VP for the Central Region for IPD, an Apollo Group subsidiary, helping with the marketing and recruitment of adult students with partner schools in Indiana, Ohio, and Kentucky. He later served Indiana Wesleyan University as VP for enrollment management and marketing and then VP for university communications. Marion College was on the verge of bankruptcy in the early 1980s before the Apollo Group's LEAP program, which Shepherd helped implement. IWU would go from some six hundred residential students and one thousand overall, to more than three thousand residential students and sixteen thousand overall—and seventeen campuses and no substantial recurring debt. Through the COVID-19 era and national economic downturn and competing local programs such as Purdue Global, IWU is navigating enrollment drops to around 12,500 (mainly due to the nontraditional program declines).

47 The Pew Research reports are much cited and easy to find, such as the 2015 report showing the pronounced drop of self-identifying Christians in America (from 78.4 percent in 2007 to

70.6 percent in 2014), the drop of mainline Protestants (from 18.1 percent in 2007 to 14.7 percent in 2014), and a similar drop among Catholics. Although the percentage of American Christians identifying with either evangelicalism or historically black traditions rose from 51 percent to 55 percent during this time, it is a "clear majority" of a shrinking base (a 0.9 percent drop out of the total population); "America's Changing Landscape," Pew Research Center, May 12, 2015, https://www.pewresearch.org/religion/2015/05/12/chapter-1-the-changing-religious-composition-of-the-u-s/. These losses are playing out in today's recruitment pools.

48   See the engaging article by Wheaton College (Ill.) alumnus and president emeritus of Missouri State University Michael T. Nietzel, "New Report: The College Enrollment Decline Worsened This Spring," *Forbes*, May 26, 2022, https://www.forbes.com/sites/michaeltnietzel/2022/05/26/new-report-the-college-enrollment-decline-has-worsened-this-spring/?sh=6df9ff1324e0.

49   See "Spring 2022 Current Term Enrollment Estimates," National Student Clearinghouse Research Center, May 26, 2022, https://nscresearchcenter.org/current-term-enrollment-estimates/.

50   "How Do You Define a 'Denomination'?" Gordon-Conwell Theological Seminary, https://www.gordonconwell.edu/center-for-global-christianity/research/quick-facts/.

51   Donavyn Coffey, "Why Does Christianity Have So Many Denominations?" *Live Science*, February 27, 2021, https://www.livescience.com/christianity-denominations.html. Complicating the discussion of denominations is whether to categorize stand-alone churches as denominations, as Howard Kramer does on his *Complete Pilgrim* site: https://thecompletepilgrim.com/americas-methodist-trail/.

52   Pastor Chris Hodges founded Church of the Highlands and remains its leader. He also founded supporting organizations GROW and ARC. See https://highlandscollege.com/about/.

53   Chris Hodges, email to the authors, July 12, 2022. We appreciate his responses to our query.

54   See https://highlandscollege.com/our-partnerships/#grow.

55   Patterson, *Shining Lights*.

56   ICEA homepage, https://www.theiceaonline.org/.

57 INCHE homepage, https://inche.one/what-is-inche.
58 CEAI homepage, https://www.ceai.org/about-us/. Its stated mission and vision: "To Encourage, Equip, and Empower Educators According to Biblical Principles" and "God's Love and Truth Transforming Our Schools."
59 IACE's homepage, https://iace.education/#about.
60 See https://www.cccu.org/about/#heading-our-work-and -mission-0.
61 See https://highlandscollege.com/about/.
62 Perry L. Glanzer, "Is the Future of Protestant Higher Education Low-Church?" *Christian Scholar's Review*, June 3, 2022, https:// christianscholars.com/is-the-future-of-protestant-higher -education-low-church/.
63 Glanzer, "Is the Future?"
64 Russell Moore, *Onward: Engaging the Culture without Losing the Gospel* (Nashville: B&H, 2015), 8 (italics original).
65 Moore, *Onward*, 8.
66 James Davison Hunter, *To Change the World: The Irony, Tragedy, and Possibility of Christianity in the Late Modern World* (New York: Oxford University Press, 2010), 257.
67 "Surviving a Culture Running from God," YouTube video, 47:25, Tony Evans sermon, posted by Tony Evans (with 630,000 subscribers as of July 11, 2022), August 4, 2021, https://www .youtube.com/watch?v=6rwqJjfJ-HE.
68 Tony Evans reflecting on the 2016 riots in his city; cited in Adelle Banks, "Tony Evans: On His New Bible and Commentary, Kirk Franklin Boycott, Wife's Health," *Religion News Service*, November 13, 2013, https://religionnews.com/2019/11/13/ tony-evans-on-his-new-bible-and-commentary-kirk-franklin -boycott-wifes-health-2-2/.
69 Moore, *Onward*, 95.
70 Moore, *Onward*, 8.
71 Wesley Seminary homepage, https://seminary.indwes.edu/about/.
72 Joel Carpenter gives a helpful overview of the growth of African Christianity and religious education: "Christian Universities Are Growing Rapidly in Africa," *University World News*, February 3, 2017, https://www.universityworldnews.com/post .php?story=20170131142300487. The label of *seminary* can be

variously defined by region and is often the equivalent of the U.S. undergraduate Christian ministries degree. See also the Center for Global Christianity and Mission, Boston University, https://www.bu.edu/cgcm/; and the Center for the Study of Global Christianity, Gordon-Conwell Theological Seminary, https://www.gordonconwell.edu/center-for-global-christianity/.

73 Glanzer, "Is the Future?"; in response to Glanzer, Hank Voss (in the comments section of the online article) comments on the health of some of these seminaries: "Fuller Seminary (some 2,000 plus graduate students), Southern Seminary (some 5,000 students), or other similar seminaries e.g., TEDS (some 2,500 students), DTS (2,400 plus students), New Orleans Baptist Theological Seminary, etc."

74 See especially his books related to this topic: Ed Stetzer, *Christians in the Age of Outrage: How to Bring Our Best When the World Is at Its Worst* (Carol Stream, Ill.: Tyndale, 2018); Stetzer et al., *The Mission of the Church: Five Views in Conversation* (Grand Rapids: Baker, 2016); Stetzer and Daniel Im, *Planting Missional Churches: Your Guide to Starting Churches That Multiply*, 2nd ed. (Nashville: B&H, 2016).

75 Michael McCormack, "In N.O., Stetzer Explains Emerging Church," *Baptist Press*, May 8, 2008, https://www.baptistpress.com/resource-library/news/in-n-o-stetzer-explains-emerging-church/.

76 Scot McKnight, "Brian McLaren's 'A New Kind of Christianity,'" *Christianity Today*, February 26, 2010, https://www.christianitytoday.com/ct/2010/march/3.59.html.

77 Perry L. Glanzer and Nathan F. Alleman, *The Outrageous Idea of Christian Teaching* (New York: Oxford University Press, 2019), 59.

78 Tony Evans Training Center homepage, https://www.tonyevanstraining.org/.

3   Collaboration

1 Bonhoeffer, "Sermon on Judges," 465.
2 Bonhoeffer, "Sermon on Judges," 465.
3 Bonhoeffer, "Sermon on Judges," 465.
4 Bonhoeffer, "Sermon on Judges," 465.

5   Bonhoeffer, "Sermon on Judges," 466.
6   Bonhoeffer, "Sermon on Judges," 466.
7   Bonhoeffer, "Sermon on Judges," 466.
8   Stanley Hauerwas, *Performing the Faith: Bonhoeffer and the Practice of Nonviolence* (Grand Rapids: Brazos, 2004), 97.
9   Hauerwas, *Performing the Faith*, 97.
10   Hauerwas, *Performing the Faith*, 99.
11   Dietrich Bonhoeffer, "Outline for a Book," in *Letters and Papers from Prison* (Minneapolis: Fortress, 2010), 503.
12   This passage is of critical importance to how the Church theologically understood the creation of man, woman, and the relationships the two were to share. Those relationships include the one forged in the sacrament of marriage and in the expression of rightly ordered sexual relations. While an important and much-debated topic at the present point in time, the scope of our study focuses on the collaborative nature of relationships men and women are to share with God and one another.
13   Adrianna J. Kezar and Jaime Lester, *Organizing Higher Education for Collaboration: A Guide for Campus Leaders* (San Francisco: Jossey-Bass, 2009), 21.
14   Kezar and Lester, *Organizing Higher Education*, 21.
15   Bonhoeffer, *Creation and Fall*, 96.
16   Bonhoeffer, *Creation and Fall*, 96.
17   Bonhoeffer, *Creation and Fall*, 96.
18   Bonhoeffer, *Creation and Fall*, 97.
19   Bonhoeffer, *Creation and Fall*, 97.
20   Bonhoeffer, *Creation and Fall*, 98.
21   Bonhoeffer, *Creation and Fall*, 98.
22   Bonhoeffer, *Creation and Fall*, 98.
23   1 Cor 13:12 (RSV).
24   Bonhoeffer, *Creation and Fall*, 99.
25   Bonhoeffer, *Creation and Fall*, 99. In this passage, Bonhoeffer was explicitly writing about Adam and Eve as theological archetypes for all humanity. The Nazis, however, would appropriate concepts such as Friedrich Nietzsche's will to power as expressions of the limitless potential represented by a super-human and a superior race. Perhaps the most thoughtful

theological critique of such an understanding is found in John Milbank's *Theology and Social Theory: Beyond Secular Reason* (Oxford, U.K.: Blackwell, 1993). In particular, Milbank argues that the logical result of a social structure defined by such a superhuman is unstable and thus facilitates ongoing ontological violence.

26 Bonhoeffer, *Creation and Fall*, 99.

27 Bonhoeffer, *Creation and Fall*, 99.

28 Aristotle and Thomas Aquinas have mixed views on humility as a virtue. In *The Road to Character* (New York: Random House, 2016), David Brooks labels humility as a central virtue and pride as a central vice. See chapter 1 of his book for further details or this brief Brooks interview with *PBS NewsHour*'s Judy Woodruff concerning the book: "David Brooks: Humility Is the Central Virtue, Pride Is the Central Vice," YouTube video, 2:10, posted by PBS NewsHour, April 15, 2015, https://www.youtube.com/watch?v=lJUc_lSRPQ0. Depending on the understanding of discipleship that animates its existence, a Christian college should assess what virtues and vices it cultivates among community members and, if needed, make adjustments.

29 The other being by royal decree, and Queen Elizabeth gave only one such designation annually during her long reign, which means that many "towns" today are exponentially larger than cathedral cities.

30 Bryan Alexander, *Academia Next: The Futures of Higher Education* (Baltimore: Johns Hopkins University Press, 2020), 165; also cf. 166–73.

31 Alexander, *Academia Next*, 166–73.

32 Boyd Taylor Coolman, *The Theology of Hugh of St. Victor: An Interpretation* (Cambridge: Cambridge University Press, 2010), 60–78.

33 This is not to overlook the strong contributions to the communities around yeshivas. See Jerry Pattengale and Timothy Dalrymple, "Higher Education 1," in *The History, Story, and Impact of the Bible*, ed. Jerry Pattengale (Washington, D.C.: Museum of the Bible, 2019), 3:7–14.

34 The authors are aware of the major theological debate over whether there is a sacred and secular, and the belief that God is over all of life. However, here we are merely using the functional terms from history.

35 See Charlemagne's *Admonitio Generalis* of A.D. 789, which reflects his desire for wide-scale education through the monasteries and religious houses—both for religious development and for practical formation (grammar and math).

36 Courtney DeMayo, "The Students of Gerbert of Aurillac's Cathedral School at Reims: An Intellectual Genealogy," *Medieval Prosopography* 27 (2012): 97–117, http://www.jstor.org/stable/44946481.

37 DeMayo, "Students of Gerbert," 99.

38 Pattengale and Dalrymple, "Higher Education 1," 3:10.

39 Although it would be an overstatement to consider the cathedral school movement as a mere business, as Douglas Jacobsen and Rhonda Hustedt Jacobsen warn against, the duel for students prompted by Peter Abelard and his former teacher is reminiscent of such; see Jacobsen and Jacobsen, *Scholarship and Christian Faith: Enlarging the Conversation* (New York: Oxford University Press, 2004), 179.

40 Todd C. Ream and Perry L. Glanzer, "The Moral Idea of a University: A Case Study," *Growth: The Journal of the Association for Christians in Student Development* 8, no. 8 (2009): 12–13. Their case study is Calvin College.

41 Perry L. Glanzer and Nathan F. Alleman, *The Outrageous Idea of Christian Teaching* (New York: Oxford University Press, 2019), 10–13.

42 Moore, *Onward*, 87.

43 See https://christianscholars.com/resources/.

44 Even some of the earliest professional societies in the mid-nineteenth century had journals.

45 C. J. Lucas, *American Higher Education: A History* (New York: Palgrave Macmillan, 2006), 36.

46 Lucas, *American Higher Education*, 119.

4 Illumination

1 Bethge, *Dietrich Bonhoeffer*, 263.

2 Joachim Hossenfelder, "The Original Guidelines of the German Faith Movement," in *A Church Undone: Documents from the German Faith Movement, 1932–1940*, ed. Mary L. Solberg (Minneapolis: Fortress, 2015), 49. Gerhard Kittel, coauthor of the still widely used *Theological Dictionary of the New Testament*, would offer an address in 1933 titled "The Jewish Question," which became a widely circulated pamphlet. Probably the most important work on the relationship many theologians shared with the Third Reich is by Robert P. Ericksen and includes his *Theologians under Hitler: Gerhard Kittel, Paul Althaus, and Emanuel Hirsch* (New Haven, Conn.: Yale University Press, 1985) and *Complicity in the Holocaust: Churches and Universities in Nazi Germany* (New York: Cambridge University Press, 2012).

3 Hossenfelder, "Original Guidelines," 50.

4 Guido Enderis. "REICH FORCES OUT CHURCH EXTREMIST; Hossenfelder, Leader of Nazi German Christians, Quits the Protestant Governing Body. COMPLETE SHAKE UP SEEN Hitler Summons Reich Bishop Mueller as New Synod to Unseat Him Is Demanded," *New York Times*, November 29, 1933, 11.

5 Shirer, *Rise and Fall*, 195. For a more in-depth historical assessment of this particular event, please see Benjamin Carter Hett's *Burning the Reichstag: An Investigation into the Third Reich's Enduring Mystery* (New York: Oxford University Press, 2014).

6 Shirer, *Rise and Fall*, 195.

7 Shirer, *Rise and Fall*, 195.

8 Bonhoeffer, "Sermon on Judges," 467.

9 Bonhoeffer, "Sermon on Judges," 467.

10 Bonhoeffer, "Sermon on Judges," 467.

11 Bonhoeffer, *Berlin*, 467.

12 Bonhoeffer, *Berlin*, 467.

13 Bonhoeffer, *Creation and Fall*, 133.

14 Bonhoeffer, *Creation and Fall*, 145 (italics original).

15 Bonhoeffer, *Creation and Fall*, 145.

16 Bonhoeffer, *Creation and Fall*, 145.

17   Bonhoeffer, *Creation and Fall*, 146.

18   Vishal Mangalwadi and David Marshall, eds., *The Third Education Revolution: Home School to Church College* (Pasadena, Calif.: Sought After Media, 2021).

19   For example, the engaging chapter in his book on the C. S. Lewis College reflects the difficulty of actualizing a concept, however well-structured it may be and whomever its progenitor. One of the authors oversaw the gifting of the D. L. Moody college campus in Northfield, Mass., after the failed launch of said college. The funders had purchased the campus for this express purpose but eventually regifted it to Grand Canyon University (which also failed to launch for a different reason—a shareholders' vote), then regifted it a third and final time: part to Aquinas College (Calif.) and part to the Moody Center. The choice of Aquinas, in essence, reflects the leanings of the C. S. Lewis model with its emphasis on a Great Books curriculum (reducing need for a wider faculty on site). John Anacker and David M. Bastedo, "C. S. Lewis College," in Mangalwadi and Marshall, *Third Education Revolution*, 223–48.

20   MacCulloch, *Christianity*, 570. An interesting contrast to the great libraries of manuscripts is found in the conclusion of this helpful book: George W. Houston, *Inside Roman Libraries: Book Collections and Their Management in Antiquity* (Chapel Hill: University of North Carolina Press, 2014), 253–64.

21   Images and details are available from the noble fragment on display at the Museum of the Bible in Washington, D.C., and highlighted in Christian Askeland, Ashley Carter, Jerry Pattengale, and Amy Van Dyke, *The Bible in the U.S. Capital* (Carol Stream, Ill.: Tyndale House/Museum of the Bible Books, 2022), 140–43.

22   One of his two-volume Bibles of 1462 (on vellum) is on display at the Museum of the Bible and highlighted in Askeland et al., *Bible in the U.S. Capital*, 84–87. It is also a chained copy from a chained library.

23   Vishal Mangalwadi, "Mastering the Media," in Mangalwadi and Marshall, *Third Education Revolution*, 654.

24   The Museum of the Bible has a collection of these and a full display on their history and usage (History Floor). See

Askeland et al., *Bible in the U.S. Capital*, for a Paris Pocket Bible (ca. 1230–1236, with marginalia).

25 See the discussion on the use of classical texts in Tina Chronopoulos' review of *The Classics in the Medieval and Renaissance Classroom: The Role of Ancient Texts in the Arts Curriculum as Revealed by Surviving Manuscripts and Early Printed Books. Disputatio, 20*, by Juanita Feros Ruys, John O. Ward, and Melanie Heyworth, *Bryn Mawr Classical Review* 32, no. 3 (2014), https://bmcr.brynmawr.edu/2014/2014.03.32/.

26 Rabbi Jacob ben Isaac Ashkenazi, quoted in Israel Zinberg, *A History of Jewish Literature: Old Yiddish Literature from Its Origins to the Haskalah Period*, trans. Bernard Martin (Cincinnati, Ohio: Hebrew Union College Press, 1975), 131.

27 The actual Royal Charter from Henry VIII was in 1534 (Letters Patent); Oxford University Press homepage, https://www.cambridge.org/our-story.

28 B. A. Uhlendorf, "The Invention of Printing and Its Spread till 1470: With Special Reference to Social and Economic Factors," *Library Quarterly: Information, Community, Policy* 2, no. 3 (1932): 187, http://www.jstor.org/stable/4301902.

29 "What Would You Fight For?" University of Notre Dame, https://fightingfor.nd.edu/.

30 "2020 'Notre Dame on NBC' Season Is Network's Most-Watched in 15 Years," NBC Press Release, November 9, 2020, https://nbcsportsgrouppressbox.com/2020/12/09/2020-notre-dame-on-nbc-season-is-networks-most-watched-in-15-years/.

31 University of Notre Dame Alumni Association, "Our Mission," https://my.nd.edu/page/home-main.

32 University of Notre Dame Alumni Association, "Season 7, Episode 7," in *Everyday Holiness Podcast*, https://faith.nd.edu/s/1210/faith/interior.aspx.

33 University of Notre Dame Alumni Association, "Daily Gospel Reflection," September 29, 2022.

34 University of Notre Dame Alumni Association, "Notre-Dame de Paris: Architecting a Legacy," September 27, 2022, https://think.nd.edu/notre-dame-de-paris-architecting-a-legacy/.

Index